# The Arabian
# English Pleasure Horse

# The Arabian English Pleasure Horse

## A Guide to Selecting, Training and Showing

KATHLEEN OBENLAND

HOWELL
BOOK HOUSE

New York

Maxwell Macmillan Canada
TORONTO

Maxwell Macmillan International
NEW YORK OXFORD SINGAPORE SYDNEY

**To Firetok**

Copyright © 1991 by Kathleen Obenland

All rights reserved. No part of this book may be reproduced or transmitted in any form or by any means, electronic or mechanical, including photocopying, recording, or by any information storage and retrieval system, without permission in writing from the Publisher.

Howell Book House
Macmillan Publishing Company
866 Third Avenue
New York, NY 10022

Maxwell Macmillan Canada, Inc.
1200 Eglinton Avenue East, Suite 200
Don Mills, Ontario M3C 3N1

Macmillan Publishing Company is part of the
Maxwell Communication Group of Companies.

Library of Congress Cataloging-in-Publication Data
Obenland, Kathleen.
    The Arabian English Pleasure horse : a guide to selecting,
training and showing / Kathleen Obenland.
        p.   cm.
    Includes index.
    ISBN 0-87605-894-2
    1. Arabian English pleasure horses.   2. Arabian English pleasure
horse class.   I. Title.
SF296.E53O24   1991
636.1'12—dc20          90-25865          CIP

Unless otherwise noted, all photographs are by the author.

Macmillan books are available at special discounts for bulk purchases for sales promotions, premiums, fund-raising, or educational use. For details, contact:

Special Sales Director
Macmillan Publishing Company
866 Third Avenue
New York, NY 10022

10 9 8 7 6 5 4 3 2 1
Printed in the United States of America

# CONTENTS

# ACKNOWLEDGMENTS

I want to thank the many people who have contributed both directly and indirectly to the making of this book, especially the tremendously talented trainer John Rannenberg for his assistance with the training chapter; trainers Jim and Peter Stachowski, Sheila Varian and Pat Richardson; my ever-patient photo assistants Bettie Towner and Dana Hensley; and farriers J. Scott Simpson and C. Jayne Brahler for their assistance with the shoeing chapter.

A special thank-you goes to my parents, Bert and Carol Obenland, who strongly supported and encouraged my horse efforts through the years, and who in their own ways have made my equine achievements possible.

# FOREWORD

ENGLISH PLEASURE IS THE MOST POPULAR of the performance classes, and the most prestigious. When the English Pleasure finals class at the Nationals goes into the ring, there is scarcely an empty seat in the coliseum. Even at smaller shows, the stands fill when the English classes are in the ring. The audience is drawn by the class's brilliance and energy. People want to be a part of that, to get behind it and support it.

To me, it is the most exciting of classes. The amount of motion we're seeing in the ring today is ideal. Horses successful in the show ring are trotting at or somewhat above level and have nice, rolling canters that show a lot of flex. That's a style we should work to maintain. If we demand more motion than that from our horses, we're going to have a hard time separating English horses from Park horses.

Of course, not all English-type horses have the motion it takes for today's English Pleasure or Park classes, but there is a place in the ring for them as well, in the Country Pleasure. This is a beautiful, elegant class that showcases the talents of this different fashion of English horse.

All of the English style classes have become extremely competitive. The quality of the horse you see in the ring today is superior to that of even fifteen years ago. In general, there has been a trend toward breeding for horses with good performance ability, but there has been particular emphasis on producing the English-type horse. Breeders today know more about producing horses that are both athletic and show good Arabian type.

Part of our ability to breed better English horses comes from breeding to produce athletes specifically suited to the task we have in mind for them. The horses are more specialized, with bodies and attitudes better suited to their jobs. The mindset of the English horse is just as important as the proper build. The great horses go into the ring giving it everything they have and at the same time make all that energy look effortless. Those are the horses you wait and watch for. They make it all worthwhile. That special quality is something they are born with, and it is as vital as it is hard to define.

I also believe that in our efforts to improve our own breed, we have benefited from opening ourselves to the ideas and practices of other breeds. Outbreeding put us in touch with trainers and breeders of other English-type horses. It let us see what they view as the characteristics of a good English horse, how they breed for that type of horse, and how they refine the horse's ability through training. This cross-pollinating of ideas has been a definite stimulant.

But the tremendously talented horses that we're seeing in the ring are only half of what it takes to make the horses successful. The team is completed by equally talented trainers, trainers who are more knowledgeable and better educated then ever before. Today's trainers are able to attain higher levels of training to develop and finely tune the abilities of the horses.

Many trainers and others knowledgeable in the field give clinics and seminars, and devote a great deal of time to English Pleasure education. In doing so, they ensure the future quality of the class, the horses and the people who ride them.

But until now, one thing had been missing—a complete, written guide to English Pleasure.

And here it is.

In a clear, easy-to-understand manner, the author covers selection, training, showing and care, and provides a wealth of information about the most popular class in the ring today. It gives the reader an inside look into everything, from what the English trainers look for in a horse to how to make the horse look his best in the show ring.

John Rannenberg

Kathleen Obenland and Firetok at the 1978 U.S. National Arabian and
Half-Arabian Championship show where they won the Arabian English Pleasure
Amateur Owner to Ride 18 and Over. Photograph by Rob Hess.

# INTRODUCTION

THERE WAS A TIME WHEN I saw English Pleasure as a matter of what saddle the horse was wearing instead of what horse was wearing the saddle.

That's about the same as saying a jogger can become a gymnast by changing shoes. To become a gymnast, the individual must have physical ability, the right attitude, and training. It is the same with English horses.

They are heat and energy and exhilaration expressed in the joy of motion. They are specialists, their natural talents honed to a fine edge with training. Like other specialists, when they reach a level of expertise they often will practice one craft and one craft only. At a regional and national level, an English horse will not be seen ridden western or hunter seat. Those styles require different talents and are practiced by horses with different builds.

Hot is in, and there are few things as exciting as riding and watching English Pleasure. At any one show, it is likely to be one of the most popular classes. For instance, at the 1989 United States Arabian and Half-Arabian Nationals, there were 385 entries in English Pleasure classes alone.

The sport is growing with the Arabian industry. In 1978 the International Arabian Horse Association had 137,822 purebred Arabians registered. In 1988 there were over 357,000. Around 25,000 purebreds and 8,000 Half-Arabians are registered annually.

English is the excitement of the breed. The search is on for horses that show the exaggerated knee and hock action of the English trot. The cost of a national-quality English Pleasure horse might range from $20,000 to more than $100,000. With prices like that, many people are looking to find or breed to produce horses with English potential.

English is in the body and mind of the horse. It is not a matter of changing the saddles, although I see this a lot at the small shows and was once a practitioner myself. It can be successful at the small shows because everyone else is doing it. It's like a human athlete entering a triathlon of swimming, bicycling and running. He may do well against others in the triathlon, but it is unlikely that he would be equally successful if he were to enter a running marathon and compete against those who make running their specialty. The higher the level of competition, the more specialized the athlete must be, whether the athlete is human or equine.

My English career started more with the saddle than with the horse. My folks bought me a saddleseat English saddle, I slapped it on the little gray Arabian I was riding western, and presto, I had an English horse. At least I thought I did. I'd never actually seen what I now consider a real English horse.

My beginning equine pursuits were less than spectacular. A riding instructor once evaluated my riding skills as "hopeless." My first horses were equally as bad and ended up with mouths like concrete.

Hopeless is not a permanent condition, however. It is a starting place. It's the beginning of dreams and goals and ambitions.

I began winning national titles in 1986, when I placed Top Ten in the nation with Natural High, a National Show Horse (an Arabian/Saddlebred cross) in Half-Arabian English Pleasure, Amateur Owner to Ride, 18 and over. In 1987 I returned to the Nationals with the love of my life, the purebred gelding Firetok, and won the national championship in English Pleasure, AOTR, 18 and over. He was five years old at the time, and it was his first season on the horse-show circuit. He gave me his best and made all the years and the work worthwhile. The following year, 1988, we went to the Canadian Nationals and captured a Top Ten title. From 1987 to 1989, Firetok won $40,000 in the show ring.

The beginning of my salvation from mediocrity was an Arabian stock horse, Takara Fadruffles (Gin), who was talented enough that it bothered me that he was more talented than I was. Equine blackmail. He lit the fire of desire to be better, to work harder, to make myself as good as he was. He started the obsession and with a number of riding instructors taught me to ride. He showed me glimpses of what was beyond the dusty arenas of little back-yard shows. He went from being my little gray 4-H go-in-every-class horse to winning national stock-horse titles in the United States and Canada.

I rode him English at small shows for a while. It was not one of his talents, but in the meantime his success in other areas carried us to shows where I could see what real English horses looked like. Before long my family purchased one, but unfortunately we made a rather bad choice. The next one was also a bad choice (we bought her based on a picture in a magazine—not one of the better horse-selection techniques a person can utilize), but the horses got increasingly better after that.

English became the contagious disease from which I did not want to be cured. It's raw excitement. You get hooked on the heat of the horses and the rush of adrenaline that pumps through you when sitting astride one or watching them go.

The things my family wished to achieve seemed quite impossible at times, but impossible is just another perception like hopeless. We started from scratch with a corral in back of the house, a spotted pony and very little money. The corral sprouted fences that extended across the land. A barn went up, then expanded. The pony gave way to an increasing quality and number of horse. Gradually, we became Southwind Arabians of Pomeroy, Washington, specializing in select English Pleasure horses.

Nothing comes overnight, but each tomorrow can bring increasingly better things if you make the effort to attain them. There may seem a tremendous chasm between the level of competition you have reached and where you dream of being. Watch those who win. If that is what you want, find the means to take you there. It may involve riding lessons, a different horse, a trainer for the horse, or all of the above. There's nothing wrong with recognizing your deficiencies and trying to overcome them. You can strive to be a little better, try a little harder and reach a little farther. It's not enough to be lucky. It is the learning and hard work that count. You will achieve your goal in the end.

# 1

# English Pleasure

AN ENGLISH PLEASURE CLASS ASKS only three things from the horse—that he be able to perform the walk, trot and canter on demand.

That is of course a great oversimplification of the class, but reduced to its most basic elements, that is what an English class is. The class may only last 15 to 20 minutes, but each of those minutes is dearly bought. Every minute is a distillation of months of training, feeding programs, proper shoeing, grooming, care, conditioning, money, frustration and elation. Most horses are in training four to six months before they enter their first class. It will be many months more before training and maturation produce a seasoned show horse that can, for each of those 15 to 20 minutes, give the kind of brilliant performance that is sought.

None of it comes quickly, but if you make your choices wisely, it will come. Even if you do not have your English horse yet, attend the shows and notice the type of horses that are competing successfully.

At the shows, the English horse is asked for the walk, trot and canter. In some classes the horse may also be asked to perform two extended gaits, the extended trot and hand gallop.

The walk is a four-beat gait, meaning that each of the four feet strikes the ground separately. At least one foot is on the ground at all times. You might be able to hear each hoof strike the ground if the horse were walking across a paved street. The American Horse Shows Association (AHSA), which writes the rules governing horse shows, describes the proper English walk as "brisk, true and flat-footed with good reach."

"Flat-footed" means the horse is walking in a normal, relaxed fashion with the heel of the foot striking the ground first, followed by the toe. He's not jigging and doesn't look like he's trying to walk on his toes or is about to explode. Of all the gaits in an English class, the walk gets the least attention. Still, it is an essential gait. Although you'll never hear the crowd whooping and yelling to see the horses walk, it nevertheless must be performed well.

If any gait dominates the class, it is the trot. The normal trot is a two-beat gait. A foreleg and the opposite hind strike the ground at the same time. At any one time there are two feet or no feet on the ground. A winning trot in the show ring is one where the horse is trotting near center or level, meaning the foreleg reaches upward, knee flexed, until it is parallel to the ground. The hind foot also should show good height of stride (see page xii). A horse moving in this fashion is said to have balanced motion and be moving square. The AHSA describes the proper normal trot as "mannerly, cadenced, balanced and free moving." It is performed with moderate speed.

The strong trot is an extension of the normal trot. Although the gait tends to be faster than the normal trot, the strong trot is not just speed. There must also be a lengthening of stride.

The canter is a three-beat gait. The horse pushes off with one hind leg, followed by the other, then the opposite front. The last leg to hit the ground indicates the lead, which should be the inside front if you are in an arena. Leads are a matter of balance for the horse. On the left lead, the left front hits the ground last, and the horse can more easily circle to the left. On the right lead, the right front hits the ground last and the horse can more easily circle to the right. When in the show ring, the horse must always have the inside lead at the

Tshannon, ridden by John Rannenberg, shows exceptional balance in her motion. Notice she has nearly as much height of stride behind as she does in front. Photograph by Rob Hess, courtesy Rohara Arabians.

canter and hand gallop. The rider directs the horse which lead to take. The wrong lead is a major error and occurs occasionally even in national competition.

The hand gallop is an extension of the canter. It is not simply a faster version of the canter. The stride must lengthen. The horse should be under control at all times, and according to the AHSA rules, extreme speed will be penalized.

Park horses also show at the walk, trot and canter, but there is a marked difference between a Park horse and an English horse. Park is a brilliant, dramatic class. The horses trot and canter way over center. It is an expression of motion in the extreme and takes tremendous exertion and talent. Quality Park horses are few and far between.

A type of English at the other end of the spectrum from Park is Country Pleasure. Country Pleasure is a class for English-type horses that do not have the extreme motion it takes for English Pleasure or Park. The Country Pleasure horse should appear elegant and fluid in his gaits and have a quiet, pleasant manner, without the jacked-up, energized look of the English Pleasure horse. County Pleasure is judged on attitude, manners, performance, quality and conformation, in that order, according to the AHSA rule book. English Pleasure horses cannot enter Country Pleasure classes, and vice versa. High, English Pleasure-type action is penalized in Country Pleasure. The Country Pleasure horse is shown at the walk, trot, extended trot, canter and hand gallop.

While the Country Pleasure horse does not need as much high action, elevation and collection as the English Pleasure horse, the selection, training and care of the two styles of horses are quite similar. The principles discussed in this book apply to both and also apply to the Half-Arabian as well as the purebred.

At all times the horse should be light on the bridle. That means there is light contact between horse's mouth and the rider's hands via the reins. The horse should not lean on the bridle or sag behind it.

All gaits in English Pleasure should be performed with collection and elevation. When collected, the horse's hindquarters are working well beneath the body instead of trailing along behind. A collected horse moves in a balanced manner and can easily execute tasks without breaking gait or skipping with a hind leg in an effort catch up with the front. The most extreme example of collection you probably have experienced is the overly excited horse that jogs or hops up and down in place. Tremendous collection of the body allows him to do it with ease.

An uncollected horse is "strung out." If asked to canter a tight circle, the canter probably would erode into a trot because the horse lacks the coordinated movement between front and rear to get the job done. An uncollected horse may overreach or interfere, striking his rear feet against his front. The horse may be clumsy and stumble. The performance in the ring will be mediocre. The walk will be lackluster, the trot will be not as high or brilliant and the canter loose. A talented horse still may look all right uncollected, but if that is true he will do far better collected. Collection brings a quality and brilliance to the gaits

4

that can boost the horse to the top of the class—which is, after all, where you strive to be.

To the rider, the collected horse feels compact. The strung-out horse feels long, as if the hind end is a considerable distance from the front. It takes practice and observation to know the difference between a horse that is collected and one that is not (see pages 3 and 6).

The extraordinary Park horse Zodiac Matador, U.S. National Champion Park in 1984, 1985 and 1987. Photograph by Rob Hess, courtesy Pinnacle Arabians.

This horse is uncollected, strung out and shows mediocre elevation. Photograph by Bettie Towner.

The same horse, now collected. Notice how much more compact he looks. His stride is higher, movement more balanced, the head is set and he presents a more pleasing picture, although he could still use more elevation. Photograph by Bettie Towner.

After collection is achieved, elevation is possible. Elevation is the lifting of the front quarters to allow them more freedom of movement. To free the front, the horse gathers the hindquarters beneath him, shifts his weight backward and drives forward. In the front quarters, the horse pulls his neck up tall, putting the weight of the neck more over the shoulders. If the neck is left hanging out in front of the horse, the weight of it hinders the freedom of movement of the front end.

To understand how this works, get down on your hands and knees. With your weight evenly distributed, pick up a hand and reach out in front of you. Now put your hand back down. Shift your weight back onto your knees, then reach forward with your hand again. You'll find it was considerably easier the second time. Now with weight even on all fours again, stretch your neck out in front of you as far as you can, then reach your arm in front of you. Difficult, isn't it? Stretching your neck forward brought your weight forward. Now pull your neck back as far as you can without tipping your head back. With your body in this position, try reaching forward with your hand again. You'll find it has become easier.

While this demonstration probably is something you only will want to do when no one is watching, it will help you understand how weight distribution affects the horse's performance. The less weight in the front, the easier it will be for the horse to attain the high, lofty trot and canter that are desired.

Another characteristic looked for in the show ring is a bright, perky, ears-forward attitude. A horse that displays this attitude is said to be "looking through the bridle."

There are a variety of classes that can be entered with an English Pleasure horse. Most call for the walk, normal trot, extended trot, canter and hand gallop. These classes include English Pleasure:

- Open   As the name suggests, this class is open to all
  English Pleasure horses. At larger shows, this class will be
  comprised mainly of professional trainers, but amateurs are
  not barred from competing.
- Stallions   Open only to stallions.
- Mares   Open only to mares.

- Geldings   Open only to geldings.
- Maiden   Open to horses that have not yet won one first-place ribbon.
- Novice   Open to horses that have not yet won three first-place ribbons.
- Limit   Open to horses that have not yet won six first-place ribbons.

English Pleasure classes in which the horses are asked for only the walk, normal trot and canter include:

- Junior Horse   Open to horses four years old and under.
- Amateur Owner to Ride   Open to amateurs riding horses they own or that are family owned. An amateur is anyone who does not receive money for training horses or giving clinics, seminars or riding lessons, according to the AHSA. Amateur classes may be broken into rider age groups such as 13 and under, 17 and under, and 18 and over. The 17 and under class also might be called Junior Amateur Owner to Ride. The 18 and over might be called Adult Amateur Owner to Ride.
- Ladies to Ride   Open only to women.
- Gentlemen to Ride   Open only to men.
- Junior Exhibitor   Open to people age 17 and under.

At the regional level, all of these classes are reduced to six: Open; Junior Horse; Amateur Owner to Ride 13 and Under, 17 and Under, Adult; and Geldings. At the Nationals are offered Open, Junior Horse, and the three amateur divisions.

# 2

# Building Motion

SUCCESS IN THE SHOW RING is not attained by good luck, but rather by having a quality horse.

No amount of time, training, money, wishes or dreams can make an untalented horse into a talented one. Look in anyone's pasture and you'll see Almost Made It and his faithful sidekicks, Zero Talent and the ever-irritating Wasted Talent. My family has owned its share of them.

"Almost" will draw hard and heavy on your pocketbook before you finally realize that he's never quite going to be what you want. We worked on our Almost for years before facing the truth that she would never be the show horse we wanted. Almost, but not quite. That doesn't mean she then had no purpose in life, just not in our lives. We sold her to someone who now is quite happy with her as a brood mare.

It's hard to decide if "Zero" is more or less frustrating than "Almost." You can spend an amazing amount of time trying to convince yourself that surely the horse must have some talent. He very well may, but unless his talent is for the use you have in mind, he should be sold to someone who will find his potential. Selling him is a hard thing to do because you may have to turn your back on all of the money you've already put into him, and price him at what he is worth, rather than what you wish he was worth. Some breeders have been known to give such horses away.

Wanting the horse to be an English horse doesn't make him one. It may be just a trail-riding horse or a 4-H horse. That·sounds very nice but is a financial nightmare to the owner who shelled out big bucks for the breeding fee and the related expenses that brought the horse into existence. It's just as bad, if not worse, if the person bought instead of bred the horse. For Zero to grow up to be something less than a high-priced show horse may seem like treachery of the worst kind. Nevertheless, he is what he is. Pumping money into training him will net you a well-trained, but still totally untalented, horse. Training can't compensate for nature's shortfall.

Nature doles out talent in excess to Wasted Talent horses—just not enough of the right kinds. These are the odd ones who have all the talent but, because of some physical or mental flaw, cannot perform in the ring. It is extremely difficult to accept their inability when they seem so capable of being all you ever dreamed of. We owned one of these horses. We bought him as a young, unbroke horse. He was supposed to have it all, and physically he did. His flaw was a mental instability that not only wasted his incredible physical talent but also rendered him useless for any purpose I can think of. We sold him for next to nothing to someone who, after hearing about his problem, was gambling that the young horse would gain mental stability as he aged.

All of these pasture fillers obviously are horses to avoid. When evaluating a horse, the starting points are structure and how the horse moves. Once the horse passes those tests, you can be concerned about other necessities.

# CONFORMATION

Before going any further, we should review the basics—what good conformation is and how it enables the horse to move. Horses with structural defects are more prone to break down, suffering the kinds

# THE SKELETON OF THE HORSE

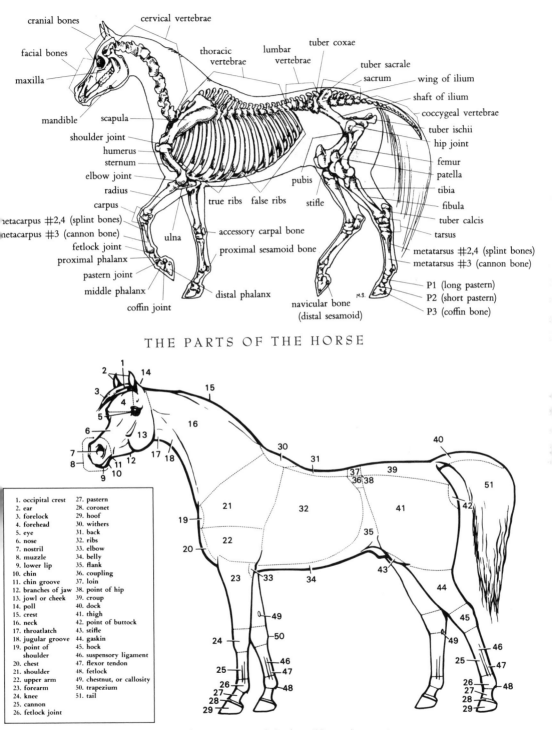

cranial bones
cervical vertebrae
facial bones
thoracic vertebrae
lumbar vertebrae
tuber coxae
maxilla
tuber sacrale
sacrum
wing of ilium
mandible
scapula
shaft of ilium
coccygeal vertebrae
shoulder joint
humerus
tuber ischii
hip joint
sternum
femur
elbow joint
patella
radius
pubis
tibia
carpus
true ribs   false ribs   stifle
fibula
metacarpus #2,4 (splint bones)
tuber calcis
metacarpus #3 (cannon bone)
accessory carpal bone
tarsus
ulna
metatarsus #2,4 (splint bones)
fetlock joint
proximal sesamoid bone
metatarsus #3 (cannon bone)
proximal phalanx
P1 (long pastern)
pastern joint
P2 (short pastern)
middle phalanx
distal phalanx
navicular bone
P3 (coffin bone)
coffin joint
(distal sesamoid)

# THE PARTS OF THE HORSE

1. occipital crest
2. ear
3. forelock
4. forehead
5. eye
6. nose
7. nostril
8. muzzle
9. lower lip
10. chin
11. chin groove
12. branches of jaw
13. jowl or cheek
14. poll
15. crest
16. neck
17. throatlatch
18. jugular groove
19. point of shoulder
20. chest
21. shoulder
22. upper arm
23. forearm
24. knee
25. cannon
26. fetlock joint
27. pastern
28. coronet
29. hoof
30. withers
31. back
32. ribs
33. elbow
34. belly
35. flank
36. coupling
37. loin
38. point of hip
39. croup
40. dock
41. thigh
42. point of buttock
43. stifle
44. gaskin
45. hock
46. suspensory ligament
47. flexor tendon
48. fetlock
49. chestnut, or callosity
50. trapezium
51. tail

Both illustrations courtesy the International Arabian Horse Association.

of injuries that put an end to show careers and drastically reduce the value of the horse.

The horse's body is supported by a skeletal structure (see page 11), and held together and driven by a network of muscles, tendons and ligaments. The brain is approximately the size of a softball.

# THE FRONT QUARTERS

The horse has the same number of vertebrae in the neck as human beings—seven. The cervical vertebrae can be compared to a flattened S. The long upper part of the S and short lower part set high onto the body create the upright posture an English horse needs to assist in lifting the front end.

If the S has poor definition, the horse will have a straight neck. This is undesirable, because it lacks elegance and refinement. If the lower part of the S is long, the horse is said to have a ewe, or upside-down, neck. A ewe neck can also result if the muscles that run from the lower jaw into the cartilage of the sternum are too coarse. The neck will bulge outward as it comes out of the chest instead of rising smoothly (see page 13). A severe ewe will make it difficult for a horse to hold his neck up and at the same time keep the head vertical, which is desired in English. A ewe neck may encourage the horse to lean on the bridle or root out his nose.

People tend to get carried away with wanting long necks. But we're talking about horses, not llamas. While a short neck may lack suppleness and be a hindrance, length isn't everything. The shape of the neck is more important than the length. A well-shaped short neck is more attractive and functional than a poorly shaped long neck. The horse uses the neck as a balancing pole. Its length must be in proportion to the body.

The cervical vertebrae are part of the spine, which runs the length of the body and is key to every movement the horse makes. The longest muscle in the body, the longissimus dorsi, ties the front quarters to the hindquarters, running from the last vertebrae of the neck to the ilium (the pelvic bone).

The front legs support 60 percent of the horse's weight. In a thousand-pound horse, that's three hundred pounds per leg, a considerable

Various structures of the neck. Top left, good neck structure for English Pleasure; top right, straight neck; bottom, ewe neck.

amount of weight. Nature has designed the leg to take the concussion and defuse it. A poorly built leg may not be able to do this properly, and the horse may go lame.

The shoulder is connected to the rest of the body only by muscle. The shoulder is comprised of two bones, the scapula and humerus, which form an angle like this: < (see page 14). The angle the two bones make gives the horse the leverage to lift his knees. Muscles at the rear of the scapula contract to rotate the top of the bone back and down. The slope of the scapula varies; 45 to 55 degrees is considered ideal.

A long humerus will increase the ease with which the horse lifts his knees, allowing higher knee action. In general, the longer and steeper the humerus, the greater the motion produced. An ideal shoulder coupled with a long humerus will give the shoulder a very angular look (see page 15). At the next show you attend, go down to the rail

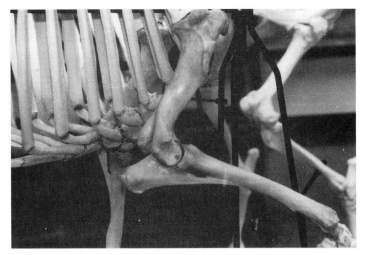
A closeup of the bones of the shoulder.

and take a good look at the English horses and the way they are built. In particular, look at their shoulders. Horses that have a lot of action up front will have angular shoulders.

Attached to the humerus are the radius and the ulna, which form the forearm. Part of the ulna forms the point of the elbow, which acts as a lever for where muscles attach. If the elbow is in extremely tight in to the body, the horse will toe out. If the elbow stands out a great distance from the body, the horse will toe in.

Below the radius is the horse's carpus (knee), which functions like the human wrist and is comprised of small, squarish bones. Below the knee is the third metacarpus (cannon bone), and beside it are the second and fourth metacarpus bones (the splint bones).

Beneath these is the proximal phalanx (pastern). Its slope should be the same as the shoulder and the angle of the hoof. Comprising part of the joint at the fetlock are two sesamoid bones, which act as levers for many of the tendons and ligaments that run down the leg.

Attached to the proximal phalanx is the middle phalanx (small pastern bone), a cube-shaped bone that allows the hoof to twist to adjust to rough ground. Beyond that bone are the navicular bone and distant phalanx (coffin bone), encased in hoof.

The skeletal structure is granted motion by a system of muscles, tendons and ligaments. The horse has no muscles below the knee. The work gets done through a network of ligaments and tendons. Ligaments connect bone to bone. Tendons connect bone to muscle. Fatigue in the muscle strains the tendons, making them prime sites for injury.

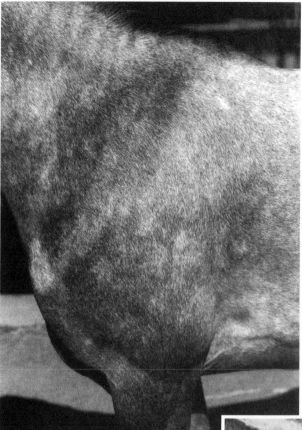

The shoulder of a national champion English Pleasure horse. Notice the angular look of the shoulder and how steep the horse is from the point of the shoulder to the point of the elbow, approximately the angle of the humerus.

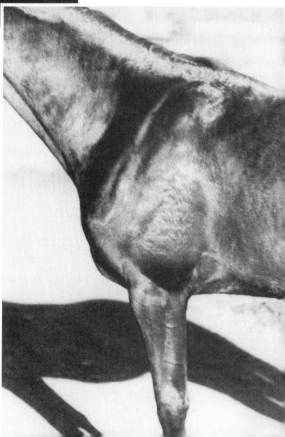

The shoulder of a Park horse with multiple national championship wins. Notice the angular look, and that the length of the humerus is even more extreme than that of the English horse.

# THE HINDQUARTERS

The hindquarters propel the horse forward and generate the lift needed for a lofty trot and canter. Weak hindquarters are a detriment to the kind of movement desirable in English.

The horse's body is made up of angles that provide leverage for movement. A level pelvis, one with a slope under 15 degrees, weakens the horse's ability to lift and drive the body forward. A flat pelvis is not the same thing as a flat croup. A flat croup is considered desirable in Arabians. A horse can have a sloped pelvis and a flat croup at the same time. The croup is the sacral vertebrae, which pass through the top of the ilium (pelvis). The pelvis is a roughly circular structure. When you place your hand on the horse's hip, you are touching a part of this bone. Viewed from the side, the pelvic bone slopes downward toward the point of the buttock.

The horse's rump should not be higher than the withers. A horse higher behind than at the withers will move as if going downhill. It will be extremely difficult for the horse to drive his rump beneath himself to lift the front end. In a young horse the rump may be higher than the withers, just as the rest of the body may grow in and out of proportion. This growing in and out of proportion usually stops at around age five. One thing that will not change as the horse grows is the conformation of the legs.

The more hind leg packed beneath the body, the sharper the angles created, and thus the more leverage for motion. A good indication of the power a horse's hind end will be able to deliver is the distance between the point of the hip and the buttocks. This distance should equal a third of the horse's body length. At the same time, the hocks should not protrude behind the point of the buttocks. A horse with the hocks far out behind him may show good English motion when trotting loose but may be unable to produce that motion under saddle. He becomes an Almost Made It or a Wasted Talent—he's got what it takes but cannot deliver under saddle because his hocks are stuck out too far behind him. He can't get them beneath himself enough to collect his body like a good show horse must.

The uppermost bone in the hind leg is the femur. It connects to the patella, then to the tibia to form the stifle joint. Below that the tibia and fibula run down toward the hock. The hock joint is comprised of six small bones arranged in three rows. The part you see as the hock is a larger bone, the calcanus (also called the os calcis). Below these are bones much like those found in the front legs. The third metatarsus (cannon), accompanied by the second and forth metatarsus (splint bones), descend from the hock joint. Below the metatarsus bones are the sesamoid bones, followed by the first, second and third phalanx (the long pastern bone, short pastern and coffin). Near the third phalanx is the navicular bone.

The horse should be longer from the hip socket to the stifle joint than from the stifle joint to the hock. This will create the desirable low-set hocks.

# SOUNDNESS

Buying the horse is just the beginning of the time and money you will spend. You want to do all you can to ensure that you're buying a horse that will be sound for many years. A horse does not have to have correct conformation to be a good English horse, but any conformation defects should not be so severe that they lead to unsoundness, alter the appearance of the gaits, or cause the horse to strike himself when moving.

Whether or not you want a horse that has ideal conformation is a matter of individual choice. However, a horse that has correct conformation has a better chance of staying sound. A horse is only as good as his feet and legs. Well-built legs distribute the horse's weight evenly, not putting more strain on one area than another. Bad conformation increases the chance that the horse may go lame under the strain of show training.

One of the easiest ways to determine good conformation is the string test. In your mind's eye, drop a weighted string from the point of shoulder. It should divide the leg and hoof into equal halves. Move that string around to the side so the tip touches the buttress of the hoof and again you should find the leg divided into equal halves. Take the string to the rear legs and drop it from the point of the buttock. It should divide the hind leg into equal halves. View this from the side, and you should find that the string is touching the horse from the hocks down to the pastern.

Deviations in the straightness of the legs will cause the legs to wing in or out when the horse moves. When the horse walks or trots toward you, the front legs should move in a straight path toward you and block out the motion of the back legs. They should not swing inward or outward as they move. As the horse moves away, the same holds true. The hind legs should move in straight paths without swinging in or out, and their motion should block out that of the front. The hind legs may, and in fact should, toe out slightly. Hind legs that are too straight are a detriment.

If you want to observe the straightness of a horse's motion, have him led toward you, then away. Watching the horse at an English trot under saddle will not give you a true picture of how straight he moves. Trotting under saddle, the front legs may seem to wobble or wing at the peak of the stride because the horse lacks the muscles in the leg to control the leg at that height.

Also when evaluating a horse's legs, look for blemishes and problems that may cause unsoundness. Many horses have blemishes that are unsightly but do not affect their soundness, for example, scars, splints and swelling. The importance in looking for them is to determine why they are there at all. Many are the results of injuries, but some may be caused by poor conformation. If you notice a conformation defect that may have caused the blemish, the blemish may be a warning. The horse may develop further problems when worked hard. On the other hand, if you are looking at a mature horse that has seen a lot of use, the blemish may be the full extent of the problems the horse will have.

Some common blemishes include:

Splints      Often appear as lumps along the inside of the leg below the knee. The bony enlargements most often occur in young horses as a result of injury or strain. The splint may be permanent or temporary depending on its severity and cause.

Windpuffs      Puffy swelling around the fetlocks, usually the result of strain put on the legs. The swelling may go down when the horse is worked or increase when he stands in his stall, or vice versa, but it is likely the swelling always will be present in some form. Unless extreme, windpuffs will not affect the horse's ability to perform.

Thoroughpin       A swelling in the sheath that contains a flexor tendon. Most appear as a soft, bulging lump above and in front of the hock. If you press on one side of a thoroughpin, it will reappear on the other side of the leg. When one first forms the horse may be lame, but later it will not be painful or cause lameness.

Among the more serious problems to look out for are those that will impair the horse's ability to perform. While the horse may have recovered from the condition, some problems can come back to haunt you. As with blemishes, it is important with some unsoundnesses to determine how they occurred. If the cause was conformation or the habits of the horse, the horse can reinjure himself again and again.
Some of the more serious problems to be on guard against include:

Bowed Tendons       These appear as a thickening or bowing out in back of the front leg and are caused by the tearing of a tendon. The thickening or bow you see is scar tissue. A bowed tendon can be caused by muscle fatigue and excessive strain on the tendon. With treatment and rest (the horse may have to be laid off for up to a year), the horse may be able to return to the show ring if the bow was mild, but the tendon never will be as good as new. In most cases, a bow is the end of the horse's athletic career.

Laminitis (Founder)       A destruction of the lamina (sensitive portion) of the hoof. It results when the horse drinks too much when hot or eats too much grain or grass. Unless the founder is severe, the horse can continue to be used, but he will be prone to founder again and may develop other problems. A horse that has been foundered may have ringed, concave hoofs and a crested neck.

Ringbone       A bony lump in the pastern area. It is serious only if it affects the joint, but the joint usually is affected.

Bone Spavin    There are many different kinds of spavins, but the bone spavin is the most serious. It is an inflammation of the bone, often in the hock. The spavin may be detectible only by X-ray. Some spavins are also detected in a test in which the hind foot is held with the foot near the belly for several minutes. The horse then will be trotted. The first few strides may be lame if the horse has a spavin.

Other spavins include bog spavin, an inflammation of the joint capsule, and occult spavin, a disease in the hock.

Club Foot    This can be inherited or be caused by injury or poor nutrition. A club foot has an angle of more than 60 degrees and may hinder the horse's athletic ability.

Before you buy any horse, have him thoroughly evaluated by a respected veterinarian. He or she has the medical training to detect problems you might not. Vet checks are standard before any purchase. Radiographs of the legs are also a good precaution. The money spent on them will be considerably less than the vet bills that might come later if you buy a horse with an unseen physical problem.

# 3

# What Trainers Look
# For in a Horse

TALENT AND QUALITY ARE THE most stunning
of attributes, and with the English horse, they are
everything. They encompass physical ability, a willingness that allows
the rider to shape that ability and the almost mystical presence that sets
the great horses apart.

In this chapter we're going to "build" the perfect English horse, the
kind English trainers dream of. Our guides on this venture are five
trainers who have spent their lifetimes seeking the ideal.

- John Rannenberg of Rohara Arabians, Orange Lake,
  Florida, has over forty horses in training at any one time.
  He is probably best known as the trainer of Canadian Love,
  1988 U.S. National Champion and Scottsdale Champion in
  English Pleasure. Rannenberg has multiple U.S. National
  and Canadian National championships, Top Tens, and
  regional wins.

John Rannenberg and Canadian Love, 1988 U.S. National Champion in English Pleasure, taking their victory lap. Photograph by Rob Hess, courtesy Rohara Arabians.

- Sheila Varian of Varian Arabians, Arroyo Grande, California, has dedicated her life to raising and training horses, including such notable horses as Bay El Bey + +, Commet + / and Huckleberry Bey + +, the sires of many successful English horses in the ring today.*
- Peter and Jim Stachowski of Stachowski Farm, Mantua, Ohio, are brothers with one of the largest Arabian training operations east of the Mississippi. It is also one of the most

*A word of explanation in about some commonly used symbols. The plus signs are given to horses that have accumulated points through showing, racing, competitive trail riding or endurance riding throughout their careers. The horse is enrolled in the program to win the title. The first is Legion of Honor (+). The Legion of Merit (+ +) has the same number of points as the Legion of Honor, but part of them must have come from halter and part from racing, competitive trail riding or endurance. The next step up in points is the Legion of Supreme Honor (+/) and the Legion of Supreme Merit (+ + +). Both of them have the

Huckleberry Bey + +, the 1984 U.S. National Reserve Champion. Huckleberry Bey is a top sire of English Pleasure horses. Photograph by Scott Trees, courtesy of Varian Arabians.

successful. Both have numerous national titles in English and Park.

- Pat Richardson of Twin Fir Arabian Stud, Sisters, Oregon, is probably best known as the trainer of *Gdansk. She devotes her time exclusively to English and Park horses, taking on only a few clients a year.

They will build for us the ideal English horse, from the head down (see page 24). When they are horse shopping, it is the horses that come closest to this ideal that are purchased. The horse must be physically able to do the task asked of him, or he cannot be successful at it. On many points, the trainers echo each other, so the general consensus is given first, under "trainers' ideal." Then matters on which the trainers disagree or have additional comments follow.

---

same number of points, but the latter earns part of the points in halter and part in performance, trail riding or endurance. The Legion of Supreme Merit is considered the highest award. Occasionally a horse will win two of these awards, like a Legion of Supreme Honor and a Legion of Merit. The symbols after the name then would look like this: + +/.

An asterisk preceding a name denotes that the horse is imported.

# HEAD

***Trainers' ideal***     The head should be appealing and obviously Arabian, with good width between the eyes. Eyes should be large and expressive, and the facial features clean and chiseled with the look of refinement. Small, shapely ears are desirable.

***Richardson***     A horse does not have to be classically beautiful to make a good performance horse. As long as the horse is not unpleasantly ugly, there is a good chance that if he moves well he will look good under saddle. The exception is a horse that is coarse. Coarseness detracts from the overall picture and can affect the horse's ability to move well.

***The Stachowskis***     A performance horse doesn't necessarily need a pretty head, but in competition beauty can give the horse a slight edge if all other things are equal. Beauty combined with ability makes for

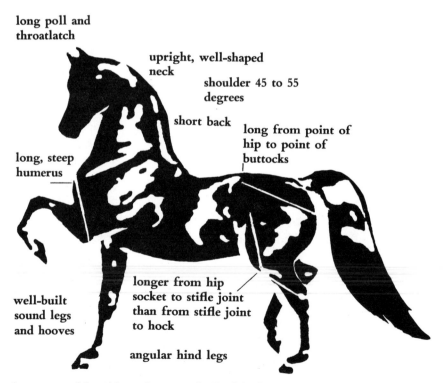

**long poll and throatlatch**

**upright, well-shaped neck**

**shoulder 45 to 55 degrees**

**short back**

**long from point of hip to point of buttocks**

**long, steep humerus**

**well-built sound legs and hooves**

**longer from hip socket to stifle joint than from stifle joint to hock**

**angular hind legs**

A summary of desirable conformation for English Pleasure.

A well-shaped neck allows the horse to bridle up tall, as seen here with RL Rah Fire, U.S. Reserve National Champion English Pleasure, 1985; also National Champion in the United States and Canada in Informal Combination, 1986. Photograph by Rob Hess, courtesy Pinnacle Arabians.

a stunning combination. A pretty head is one of the elements that adds up to an overall pleasing picture.

*Rannenberg*    A plain head detracts from the horse's appeal. A dished face is not necessary, but a head that more closely resembles Arabian type is preferable. The jaw should not be heavy or coarse. When the head is set vertically, as in the bridle, a heavy jaw can interfere with breathing and be uncomfortable for the horse. You will have difficulty setting his head.

*Varian*    A horse should have a lot of expression in its face. He should be bright, alert and showing a lot of interest in what is going on around him. It is desirable that the horse have an attractive head, but it does not have to be classic Arabian type.

# NECK

*Trainers' ideal*    The poll and throatlatch should be long, blending smoothly into a neck with good length that rises high out of the shoulders.

*Varian*    There should be suppleness in the poll and neck. Even long polls and necks can be stiff. Suppleness is more important than length. The neck also should hinge well with the head, so that it appears it will be easy for the horse to set his head high (see above).

He should carry his neck in a high, happy manner. A neck without a bow on the underside (called ewe neck or upside-down neck) is preferable. In Varian's breeding program, she was worked to breed out the ewe neck characteristic.

***Richardson and Rannenberg***    The ewe neck is not good neck structure, but these necks still can function well if the throatlatch and poll are long enough and the rest of the overall structure is good. The neck should be erect, long and with good shape. Shape is more important than length.

***The Stachowskis***    The ewe neck is not detrimental. More important is the erectness of the neck. The horse has to be able to pull his neck up tall, so that he can elevate himself to produce a big, bold trot. If his neck just hangs out in front of him, it will weigh down the front quarters, hindering elevation.

# SHOULDERS

***Trainers' ideal***    Shoulders should be angular looking. The slope from the withers to the point of the shoulder should be around 45 degrees. It should blend well into the neck and back. The shoulders receive a lot of attention from English consignors.

***Varian***    The shoulders should appear defined and refined—not meaty looking. The elbow should stand out from the horse's body enough so you can slide your hand in between the elbow and the girth (see page 27). If the elbow is in too tight to the body, it will conflict with the elbow's movement.

***Richardson***    There should be at least six inches from the point of the elbow to the point of the shoulder. That is where the humerus lies, the key to leverage that lifts the leg. The angle from point of the shoulder to the point of the elbow should be at least 45 degrees. Shoulders built like this look quite angular, and the leg may appear set well beneath the horse.

***Rannenberg***    Extremely steep shoulders translate to shorter strides, hindering the horse's ability to extend his gaits. The horse also will be rough to ride, and the pounding nature of his gaits raises concerns about future soundness. More laid-back shoulders give a smoother ride and contribute to the loose, round motion you want in English.

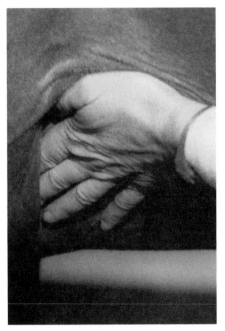

The horse's elbow should stand out far enough from the body to allow a hand to slip between them.

# FRONT LEGS

***Trainers' Ideal***    The legs should have good length. Many Arabians are a little short-legged. The forearms should be long and cannons short. Large knees should sit squarely on the legs, and the pasterns should be long and sloping.

***Varian and the Stachowskis***    Common leg problems seen among Arabians are knees that are twisted, offset or too small to support the weight of the horse. Such knees can cause perpetual leg problems. Varian is more particular about the conformation of her English horses than of her halter horses. English horses take a considerable investment in training time, and good conformation is vital in keeping the horses sound.

***Rannenberg***    Healthy, properly shaped hoofs are essential to absorb concussion. Many horses have at least one hoof that is at a different angle from the others, is dished, or has some other abnormality. Club feet particularly are to be avoided. You want a horse that has a solid, rounded hoof with angles that are the same as the angles of the pastern.

He also seeks conformationally correct horses to ward off future lameness. It is particularly important that the horse's conformational defects do not cause him to interfere. The pain of repeatedly hitting himself will make the horse difficult to train.

**Richardson**     Correct conformation is not of great concern as long as the flaws in conformation do not cause interference or changes in the appearance of the gaits. The horse can be so far off conformationally that the appearance of the gait may be altered, such as with a horse that wings excessively with one leg but not the other.

# BACK

**Trainers' ideal**     The back should be short and in proportion to leg length and the rest of the body.

**Varian and the Stachowskis**     The desirable length for a horse's back depends on the rest of the body. A balanced horse can be divided into three equal circles—the first around the shoulders, the second around the barrel and the third around the hindquarters (see below). If the back is longer than the other two units, the horse will have trouble collecting himself. And while a short back is desirable, if it is too short in relation to the legs, the horse will interfere.

A horse with balanced structure can be divided into three equal circles—the first around the shoulders, the second around the barrel and the third around the hindquarters.

*Richardson*      Horses with longer backs tend to have longer strides, but the shorter back is preferred for a number of reasons. The short back aids in collection and the leverage needed to lift the front quarters for elevated gaits. With a long back, the distance is longer between the front end that needs elevating and the rear end that is driving it forward, so there is less leverage.

*Rannenberg*      The longer-backed horse will have a harder time of it than a shorter-backed horse, but if he has good strong hindquarters and uses his hocks well, his performance still can be quite exceptional.

# HINDQUARTERS

*Trainers' ideal*      The hindquarters provide the power to drive the horse forward, so they must be strong. The croup should be long. Flat croups, while desirable in halter horses, are not necessary in performance horses. The horse also should be long from the point of the hip to the point of the buttocks. The hocks should be low set.

*Varian:*      Look for deep muscling on the hindquarters. It doesn't have to be heavy, but the muscle must carry well down into the hind leg. Joints should be good-sized and without puffiness.

*Richardson*      The angle created by the line from the point of the hip to the point of the buttocks should be about the same as the angle of the shoulder, around 45 degrees.

*Rannenberg*      The horse also should be long from the point of the hip to the point of the buttocks. Long hips give strength and power. A horse with shallow, short hips will lack the ability to drive himself forward well.

Avoid horses that are canted out—hocks protruding beyond the point of the buttocks. These horses, while they may appear to move well free, can lose much of their motion under saddle. Collection is extremely difficult for them.

The horse should appear to have a lot of hind leg packed beneath him, but the hocks should not protrude. The legs will have a very angular look to them. If the hind legs are too straight, lacking that angular look, the horse will have difficulty delivering the powerful drive you need. The angles produce the leverage for power. The horse has to be able to drop his hindquarters down and collect himself. Too many English horses have extreme motion in front but little behind.

# OTHER

***Trainers' ideal***     There is a trend toward wanting horses that are large, but size has little to do with the outcome of the class. Aesthetically, it also is desirable that the horse carry his tail high and straight. The desirable color is a matter of taste.

# MOTION UNDER SADDLE

***Trainers' ideal***     The horse should pull his neck up tall, and drive forward with strong hock action. In front, he should trot at or over level, meaning the forearm extends upward until it is parallel to the ground (see page 31). The motion is round. The horse should not flip his leg out like he is throwing a Frisbee. He also should not pump his legs frantically up and down like they are trapped inside an invisible box. That is considered "trappy." The horse must be able to extend beyond the confines of the box.

***Richardson***     A good English horse will move at every gait with a lot of flexibility and bend of the knee and fetlock joints. As the horse moves, the knee should bend first, then the fetlock joint in a round motion like a wheel (see page 31). The hoof should come down following the same circular motion. The way a horse walks may reveal his potential to move well under saddle. Watching an English class, you may notice the majority of the top horses will have a backward flip or snap to the motion of their hoofs as they pick them up at the walk. The fetlock and knee also seem to curl or fold, as if with more effort the horse could touch the hoof to the back of his leg. At the trot, this folding elongates, is given height and becomes the English trot.

***The Stachowskis***     Look for that folding in front and a lot of looseness and flexibility in the movement of the hindquarters, particularly the hocks. If the horse is stiff behind, he will not be able to generate the kind of English motion desired. Some horses have a lot of motion in front but not behind. That is not a balanced way of going. The motion behind should nearly match that in front (see page 32).

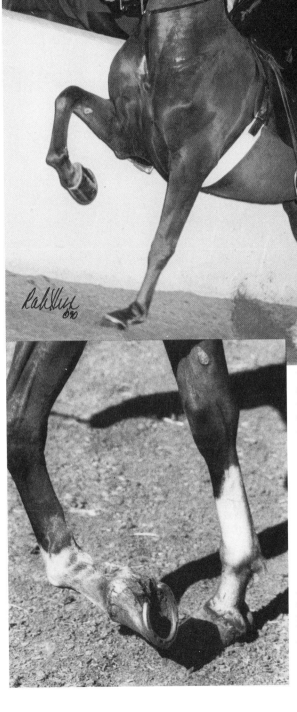

WN Astra, 1990 Scottsdale Champion in English Pleasure, under the direction of rider Joey Canda. Photograph by Rob Hess, courtesy Southwind Arabians.

As the horse moves, the knee should bend first, then the fetlock, in a round motion like a wheel. The horse should appear loose and flexible even at the walk.

Motion in front should nearly match that behind. This is Basks Last Love, U.S. National Champion English Pleasure, 1987. Photograph by Rob Hess, courtesy Pinnacle Arabians.

***Rannenberg***     Strides should be even with each other. Look out for horses that have a longer stride on one side than the other or have a hitch in their movement. It is an indication there is something wrong. Some horses are lame, hurting or on medication.

At the canter the horse should have rolling motion with a lot of flex to the knees. The old saying that the canter should feel like sitting in a rocking chair is true. A horse that springs along stiff like a deer will trot the same stiff way.

The horse should perform all gaits with steadiness and consistency. Steadiness means the head does not bob or move around, strides are of equal length and height and speed is consistent. He should not lose collection or fade in the corners.

***Varian***     At all gaits the horse also should have an overall balanced appearance. The more natural balance he has, the easier it is for him to perform under saddle. In the ring he should have a bright attitude, looking where he's going. His overall appearance should leave the impression of brightness, pleasantness and ease.

# MOTION IN GREEN HORSES

*Trainers' ideal*     In the early stages of training, horses often show little of the motion they will have as finished horses. They also are considerably less expensive than finished horses. To know if you are getting a good buy or just another decoration for the pasture, consider the horse's age and time under saddle in relation to the motion you are seeing. Look for the basics of athletic ability, good fold to the legs, a tendency to use the hocks well, overall carriage and the conformation that produces motion. You may also want to ask to see him turned loose.

*Richardson*     A horse that is three to four years old and in the first year of training lacks not only the training of a mature horse, but also muscle control and development as well. He will not be capable of the height of stride or the balance of the mature horse. Because his mind is as young as his body, his attention span is limited. As he reaches his second and third year of training, his muscles will define for the action and collection demanded of him (see page 34).

*Rannenberg*     With a green horse, try to imagine what more training, time and conditioning will do for him. Does the horse appear to have the physical ability to do the work? Does he look comfortable, or strained? If he is showing strain already, he may have some physical or mental problem that will prevent him from being what you want him to be. Is he moving forward nicely? Does he have a roundness to his trot and canter that with training can be developed and lifted? Be wary of a horse that moves stiffly.

*The Stachowskis*     Also consider what is being done to the horse, and how he is responding to it. If the horse is being pushed hard, already has a good head set, and appears to be balanced and is doing almost everything right, the motion you see is about all you'll get. The horse has had enough training to be able to show what kind of motion he has, although a little more will come with maturity. On the other hand, if you see a horse that is at a lesser stage of training, and perhaps is leaning on the bridle or is uncollected or having other difficulties, he probably is capable of much more motion. He simply lacks training and maturity.

33

Sometimes when you go to see a horse, props such as shakers (bottles full of rocks rattled) will be used on him. It excites the horse, making him look and move better. That's fine, but you'll want to see what he looks like without them, too. The props create an illusion, and you can't ride illusion into the ring.

A young horse is not capable of as great a height of stride and collection as it will have as a mature horse. This is Twice the Fire early in her show career. Photograph by Rob Hess, courtesy Twin Fir Arabian Stud.

Twice the Fire as a mature, finished show horse. Notice how much more balanced she is than in the earlier picture. She is much more elevated, trotting higher and using her hocks better. Photograph courtesy Howard Schatzberg, courtesy Twin Fir Arabian Stud.

# MOTION OF THE LOOSE HORSE

***Trainers' ideal***    The motion of a loose horse is difficult to evaluate, but with an unbroke horse, that is about the only view of the horse's motion you will get. The horse should demonstrate athletic ability. He should be able to pull his neck up tall, drop his hocks down beneath him and drive forward. He may or may not exhibit much trot, but he must have the looseness of movement and the ability to fold that has been discussed (see page 36).

***Varian***    Watch how the horse departs from a standing position into a trot. If he can just bounce right into it and you see strength in his movements, there may be some athletic ability there. Sometimes you can get a glimpse of his talents as he gathers himself to come out of a corner. You may see two or three strides of a really outstanding trot, which tells you the horse may have some good capabilities. He should have a suppleness in his neck and a free way of moving.

***Richardson***    Be wary of the horse that as he trots holds his neck out in front of himself like a goose. Chances are he moves that way because his hocks are set too far out behind his body. He may show impressive action, but he won't be able to give it to you under saddle when you try to jack up his neck and drive his hocks beneath him. When a horse trots loose, it shouldn't look like the hocks are working way behind him.

Watch the way the horse uses his shoulders. The shoulder should move forward, then upward. If it does not, under saddle the horse's English motion may disappear. Many horses have shoulders that simply rotate forward but not upward. They do not make good English horses.

***Rannenberg***    Most horses show mediocre action loose. That doesn't mean they will not make good English horses. Many of the high-powered horses show very little motion when they are not under saddle. Canadian Love is like that. When they are loose, they are not sufficiently collected most of the time to produce the motion you might expect. You have to watch for the quick glimpses here and there of what his under-saddle motion may be like.

Even a talented horse might not show much trot loose, but many still will exhibit good fold, as seen here at the trot. Under saddle and collected, this horse should make quite an English horse.

Also consider the pedigree. Does the horse come from a line known to produce English horses? Were the dam and sire English horses, or the granddams and grandsires, or have other horses with related pedigrees been successful in English? Horses from bloodlines not known for producing English horses are risky prospects. Also be on the lookout for horses that jazz up easily and have a lot of pizzazz, but exhibit little athletic ability. Turned loose, almost any horse can look impressive for a short time.

***The Stachowskis***    Consider how the horse is being shown to you. If he is in tall grass, deep shavings or straw, he's going to pick his feet up higher. His English trot might just be illusion. He also might have just spent the last five days locked in his stall. Any horse can look flashy after being confined for days. See if the horse still has spunk and spontaneity after he has been out for a time. Watch his movement in a relaxed situation. The use of shakers to whiz him up are okay for a few passes, just to see what he is capable of, but you also want to see him natural, without all the props.

# ATTITUDE

***Trainers' ideal***    Attitude makes the difference between the horse that can go to the top and one that will never quite make it. The horse should exhibit brightness, enjoyment of the task and a willingness to work. There is also an indefinable quality linked to this, which makes the great horses stand apart. It is that "look at me" quality that, if you were to walk out in a pasture among a hundred bay horses, would draw your attention to one specific horse.

*Varian*     Just because a horse is capable of English-type motion does not mean he has it in his heart to be an English horse. He can have every talent and capability and simply not want to go English. Trying to force him into it may cause him a great deal of stress and make him difficult to train. His performance in the ring will look forced and strained.

You may be able to get some indication of how well the horse will take to training by investigating his dam and sire. Had both been trained in English? If the willingness to go English existed in them, it probably will be present in the offspring.

*The Stachowskis*     A horse with English ability can be held back by a poor attitude. The problem might not even surface until the horse has been in training for a time. The horse reaches a certain plateau in training and stays there. You know he can do better, but he never does. Even if he reaches a stage that he can be shown, he may lack presence and never reach full potential.

*Rannenberg*     The truly great horses have that essential hard-to-define quality that turns the judges' heads. They try harder, burn brighter and give more of themselves. A bright, willing attitude can make the small horse look big and bold. A good attitude can cover a range of minor physical problems or a lack of beauty.

The horse also should have a high energy level without being mindlessly hot. A good English horse is sensible. The energy is essential to sustain a high level of performance through the class, but you have to be able to channel that energy.

# HORSES FOR AMATEURS

*Trainers' ideal*     Since the amateur rider usually is not as consistent or skilled as the professional, a horse for an amateur has to be all the things already discussed, only more so. He has to be talented, consistent, well schooled and willing to the point that he will not fall apart the moment the trainer dismounts. The best amateur horse performs to the trainer's standards long after the amateur has mounted.

***The Stachowskis*** There was a time when the horses in amateur classes were lesser than those ridden in open English by the professionals. That is no longer true. Many of the amateur horses successful today could succeed in open classes. In fact, many people shopping for amateur horses buy horses that have already been shown successfully in open. The amateur will have an easier job of it if the horse is seasoned, willing and extremely talented.

With a skilled rider, the horse will excel. With a rider who is mediocre, he will not be as good, but still can do well.

# GIMMICKS

***Trainers' ideal*** Buy a horse that does not require gimmicks to perform well.

***Richardson*** When shopping for a horse of any age, note how the horse is shod. Make sure you're looking at a horse shod within the legal weight limit. Heavier shoes make a horse trot higher, but when you show the horse you will have to stay within the legal limits or be disqualified. Look for welded areas on the shoe where lead could be hidden.

Also take note of the length of toe, which should be no longer than 4½ inches. This also influences motion. A long foot, especially if combined with a low heel, can increase motion. The low heel stresses the back of the leg, causing pain and making the horse put more effort into the strides. It also can cause him to go lame. Take the horse home and shoe him properly, and you might find his motion a mere shadow of what it was when he was shod improperly.

A good performance horse does not need gimmicks. You do not want a horse that relies on something you cannot use in the ring.

***Varian*** When shopping for a horse, also consider the environment the horse is living in, since it has a direct bearing on his mental well-being. Are the horses bitted up extremely tight and left in stalls? Are there turnout areas for the horses, or are they kept in stalls all the time? The ideal environment is relaxed and comfortable for the horse.

# 4

# Choosing a Trainer

SUCCESS IN THE SHOW RING has many components. One is a talented horse. Equally important is a talented trainer.

If you do not believe you are the best person to train your horse, consider hiring someone who is. A trainer can teach the green horse what being a show horse is all about and keep the finished horse looking sharp after the show. Many trainers also give riding lessons, which can help both you and your horse to perform at higher levels.

It can take nearly as much time to shop for the right trainer as it does to find the right horse. Go at it no less seriously than you would if you were picking a tutor for your child. Occasionally you may make a mistake and go with the wrong trainer, but given the numbers of trainers out there, you should be able to find one who will deal with you fairly and do your horse justice.

To select a trainer, first consider what expectations you have for the horse. That will narrow down the field of trainers. Does the horse have the ability to do well at local shows? Regional championships? The United States or Canadian Nationals? You need a trainer who matches your level of expectations and the ability of the horse. Someone who would be a proficient trainer for small shows might not have the necessary talent to raise the horse to the level of national competition.

If the horse fails to meet your expectations, it might be that the horse was not as talented as you first believed. Try not to be deluded by your ambitions. If your faith in the horse is absolute, however, the horse's failure to excel might mean you need a different trainer. Horses are individuals. It is unrealistic to believe that every horse will get along with every trainer.

The trainer you hire should be skilled in the class in which you want the horse trained. Although many trainers have a variety of talents, they tend to specialize. For your English horse, find an English trainer. One of the best ways to find a trainer is to attend the shows and watch the classes. Who is riding the horses you admire? Whose horses perform consistently well? Performing well does not necessarily mean the horses win all the time, but that you like their way of going, willingness and brightness. Talk to other horse owners about trainers. The owners who have been around a while can tell you about the talents and drawbacks of the trainers. Some of what you will hear will be nothing more than rumors, but talking to a lot of people at shows will give you an idea of which trainers to approach. You need a trainer whose views match your own, or you may be unhappy with the methods used to get the results you want.

Talk to the trainers, visit the barns and ask about prices. Costs vary greatly. To pay between $400 and $600 for board and training is common. At some facilities, the monthly bill will top $1,000. Your choice of trainer may be limited by the distance of the trainer from you, the cost or who will take your horse in training.

## INTERVIEWING THE TRAINER

When you meet a trainer and want to evaluate him or her, the following questions may help:

- What is the trainer's background and qualifications?
- What are the trainer's future career plans? Trainers can burn out, just like everyone else. My family once used a trainer who dropped out of the horse business to sell shoes. You want a trainer who is serious about the horse industry and wants to remain active in it. Training should not be a temporary job to tide someone over until a better job comes along.
- How many horses does the trainer have in training? The number of horses has little relation to quality of training, but it will give you an idea of the scope of the trainer's operation.
- Who are the trainer's other clients? This is like asking for references. If you have any doubts, it will give you someone to ask about the trainer's skills.
- What is the trainer's opinion of the horse's talents? If the trainer seems indifferent about taking your horse, take the horse to another trainer. Some trainers will take the horse for an evaluation period, such as sixty days. At the end of that time, the trainer can tell you if in his or her opinion the horse is going to make it. If the trainer does not have a set program for evaluations, ask how long it will be before he or she can tell you if the horse is going to be worth training. Two months' time should be sufficient for most horses.

  If it is the trainer's opinion the horse doesn't have the necessary talent, you might seek a second opinion or change your expectations for the horse. Perhaps he would make a better Western horse or stock horse than an English horse. Perhaps he lacks the talent to be one of them, but would do well at small shows or as a 4-H horse. Maybe he'll just be a saddle horse. If he's not going to make it, don't keep pumping money into him. The investment will not be worth it.
- Would the trainer be willing to show the horse? If so, where? This question is a lot like the preceding one, only it goes a step further. This will help you gauge just how

serious the trainer is about your horse. A quality trainer does not want to be seen showing a poor-quality horse.

- What are the trainer's fees, and what do they include? Most likely they will include board and training. You probably will be billed separately for veterinary services and farrier work. There can also be a range of other fees in addition to the basic rate. Ask what the average costs are for one horse at the facility.
- Does the trainer have any requirements before a horse is allowed in the barn, such as vaccinations or insurance?
- What will be done with your horse? The trainer should be able to tell you the basic approach that will be taken with the horse.
- Who will be working your horse? The trainer may or may not be working the horse personally. Many trainers have apprentices or assistants who will work some of the horses. Some trainers have the assistants do the initial breaking and starting of the horses, then they themselves do the finishing. It is perfectly acceptable to have the assistant or apprentice working your horse. Just make sure that if the helper is working your horse you know it, and that the trainer can assure you of the person's qualifications.

   If the trainer is working your horse personally and the horse is too young to be shown, ask what will be done with your horse when the trainer is at the shows. Trainers can be gone to shows for weeks at a time.
- How long does the trainer expect it will be before the horse will be able to attend a show? Horses progress at different rates, but the trainer probably will be able to give you a fairly close estimate after having the horse for a time.
- Does the trainer offer riding lessons if you want them, and is there a fee for them? Some trainers are as skilled in training people as horses. Others are not. The ability to train a horse does not make the person instantly into a teacher, and some skilled teachers would make poor trainers. You may have to hire two people—one to train you and one to train the horse.

- What expectations does the trainer have of you? This could be almost anything. He or she may expect you to pay for show expenses in advance, participate in advertising campaigns for the training facility, make your horse available for open houses at the facility, be willing to campaign the horse to the regionals or nationals if the horse has the ability, leave your horse at the facility all year or use the trainer as your agent when selling the horse.
- What stabling options are available for the horse? There may be standard stalls, stalls with paddock runs, paddocks without stalls, or pasture. The last option is unusual for a horse in training because the trainer will want to have the horse closer at hand than that. If the horse is to be kept in a stall without access to the outside, ask if the horse is ever turned out, and how often. It is important to the horse's mental well-being to be able to have some time to himself to play in a paddock, arena or pasture. Although it is good for the horse to be able to have some access to the outside, be aware that the sun will dull the shine of the horse's coat. The hair gets sunburned, giving it a fuzzy, reddish look. Light-colored horses are especially vulnerable to this. Exposed skin, such as that on the nose, can burn as well, especially if it is pink.
- Who owns the barn the trainer is working out of, and what is the trainer's relationship with that person? Many trainers work out of barns that are not their own. They may be employees of the barn owner or rent the stall space.
- Does the trainer, to the best of his or her knowledge, plan to stay at that barn? Some trainers move frequently. If you pick a trainer because he or she is within driving distance, you need to know if that person has plans to move four states away shortly after you put your horse in training.

## SHOW-RELATED MATTERS

Once you are satisfied with your trainer and your horse's progress, you'll want to discuss showing. These are some of the questions that you'll probably want to ask:

- What are the fees associated with showing the horse? These may include hauling at from 25 to 50 cents or more a mile; grooming fees and other preparation fees; a fee for every class in which the trainer rides your horse; regular show fees such as entry fees and stall rental; your share of what it costs to rent the room for grooming and tack (the price is usually divided among all the owners of the horses the trainer brings); and your share of the trainer's expenses, such as food and lodging. These fees vary from trainer to trainer. If you want to save money, the trainer might allow you to provide some of these services yourself.

- What commitments does the trainer have to show other horses? A trainer committed to ride someone else's horse in a class can't ride yours in the same class. It's physically impossible, since all of the horses are in the ring at once. This doesn't become much of a concern until the horse is ready for serious competition, but when he is ready you'll want to know if the trainer is going to be able to ride him.

- Is there anything you should be aware of that would keep the trainer from showing your horse on any given day? A trainer might not be able to show on certain days for any number of reasons, including religious obligations.

- What shows does the trainer plan on attending, and is the trainer willing to go to additional shows that you might want to attend?

- When the horse is at the show, will the time he is there be deducted from the boarding bill at the trainer's stable? Most likely it will not be.

- What are the trainer's opinions of your taking the horse to shows without him or her, or taking the horse home for periods of time? Some trainers frown on this. As the owner, you can do anything you want with the horse, but points such as this may cause friction between you. If you have a contract with the trainer, spell this out in it. When hiring a trainer, it's usually best to have a contract. If neither of you believes a contract is necessary, at least make sure he or she understands your plans for the horse.

# GETTING ALONG WITH THE TRAINER

Good relations with the trainer can be maintained if you work at it and if you have selected a compatible trainer. The following will also help:

- Always pay your bills on time.
- Make sure you agree with the trainer's methods before you hire him or her, otherwise this can become a trouble spot. Go into the relationship with your eyes open. There probably is not a trainer alive who has not been told at one point, "Now, I don't want you to hit him, because he's very sweet." That is an unreasonable request for most trainers. The horse will be pulled, kicked by the rider and struck. It is up to you to decide if the trainer is punishing the horse constructively or if he or she is being abusive, as you define the term. Pick a trainer who does what you approve of. It is unrealistic to believe you can change the trainer's methods of working the horse. Be wary of trainers who will not let you watch them work your horse.
- Remember that rushing the trainer is rushing the horse. The horse has to progress at his own pace, and rushing him will cause stress and contribute to early burnout. It is not practical to expect the horse to be in the show ring a few months after breaking. Doing it right takes time. Many horses can be in the ring in six to eight months, but there are exceptions. Horses that are difficult or mentally immature are going to take longer than horses that are receptive to training. If the trainer fails to get results, however, there may be a problem with the horse or the trainer's techniques.
- Talk to the trainer about your expectations and goals. If you will be satisfied with nothing less than a horse that is a national contender, the trainer needs to know it. The trainer's evaluation of your horse will be based upon it.

45

When the trainer tells you your horse will or will not make it, that means the horse will or will not fulfill your expectations. The trainer cannot do the job properly if he or she doesn't know your definition of what the job is.

- Keep on top of the horse's condition and how he is progressing. Insist that the trainer notify you if the horse becomes injured or ill. You may also want to pay an occasional unscheduled visit to the barn to make sure all is well. If you do make an unscheduled visit, don't expect to take up much of the trainer's time.

Even when the horse is away from home, you are the guardian of his health. You may prefer to have the trainer check with you before administering any drugs except standard maintenance medications such as dewormers.

Medications such as painkillers allow a horse to be ridden following an injury. The medication masks symptoms, and symptoms are the body's message that all is not well. The medication may help the horse in pain perform, but it may also be masking a significant problem. This is not to say that medications such as bute (phenylbuteazone) are bad; you just want to be consulted before your horse is given them.

- Recognize that you need to give the trainer time to do his or her job. While it is essential to discuss plans and goals with the trainer, there is a time and a place for it. That time is not in the middle of the rush to prepare for a class, or while the trainer is busy with other people.
- Let the trainer know you appreciate his or her efforts. If the trainer is doing a good job, say so.
- Recognize that the trainer is the specialist and that as a specialist may know more about the abilities of your horse than you do. As the owner, you may be seeing the horse as much more, or perhaps less, than he really is.

# SIGNS OF TROUBLE

There may come a time when you realize that you have picked the wrong trainer, or that the trainer who has done well for you in the past is no longer able to do the job. Trainers have problems, too, and sometimes you can stand by and wait for them to overcome them. But if a trainer's problems become severe, then it is not in the best interests of you or your horse, and you should look elsewhere. Some signs that may indicate problems with the trainer include:

- The horse is not progressing at the rate he should.
- The horse is in poor physical condition.
- The horse is showing signs of abuse. These can include unexplained injuries or marks on his body; stress-related behaviors such as weaving or windsucking in a horse that has not displayed such behaviors before; obvious fear of the trainer. Be concerned if a horse in the trainer's care has been disqualified from competition because illegal drugs or illegal devices have been used. Avoid any trainer who has been found by the American Horse Shows Association to have abused a horse. The next horse abused could easily be yours. AHSA's definitions of abuse include excessive use of the whip, using firecrackers and other explosives and rapping the horse's legs with the blunt end of a whip or other implement. Getting involved with an abusive trainer not only could be harmful to your horse but also to you. While some penalties for abuse are light, AHSA has the authority to suspend the trainer and *every* horse in the trainer's barn from competition for as long as it sees fit. All of the horses you have with the trainer could be barred from competition, even if they were not the objects of the abuse. The AHSA can also suspend all the barn's volunteers and employees, and bar anyone from showing for the trainer during the suspension. The AHSA can also expel the trainer from the organization and/or levy fines.
- The trainer consistently brings excuses, instead of your horse, to shows where he was to be shown.
- The trainer becomes defensive when you ask questions about training techniques, how the horse is shod, marks that appear on the horse's body, etc. The trainer should be able to answer your questions easily. If he or she gets upset or defensive, something's wrong.

- You frequently see the trainer drinking, drunk or high. You don't want a person who abuses alcohol or drugs to be in charge of the care and training of your horse.
- A trainer who usually comes to a show with one or more grooms instead comes solo, but brings a lot of horses. It could be that the way the classes are spaced allows the trainer to do all the work himself or herself. But if it happens frequently, it could be a sign that the trainer's program is deteriorating.
- You frequently hear bad things about the trainer's techniques or treatment of the horses. Check out these rumors where possible. Ask the trainer's other clients if they are satisfied with the care and training their horses receive.
- The trainer frequently seems moody or volatile. The trainer could be equally as bad-tempered with your horse.
- When you go to check on the horse's progress, the trainer relies heavily on devices, such as firecrackers and chains around the fetlocks, to show you how well the horse is doing. The horse can't be doing all that well or he wouldn't need them. Such devices might give you a glimpse of what the horse is capable of, but you also want to see what he is doing without all the glitz.

A good relationship with a trainer involves your finding one who will fulfill your needs, be honest with you, be concerned about what is best for the horse and recognize that he or she is working for you, not the other way around. You are entrusting your horse's mental and physical well-being and his future to this person. Choose carefully. Don't tolerate dishonesty or games. There *are* good trainers, so don't waste your time on the ones who are not. Finding a quality trainer is as important as having a talented horse. The three of you—owner, horse and trainer—are equal partners to success in the show ring.

# 5

# Tack, Bits,
# Equipment and
# Devices

THROUGHOUT YOUR HORSE'S show career, many aids will be used to help improve his skills and tune him to the rider's needs. As the owner or trainer, it's helpful for you to understand what the aids are and how they affect the horse.

## SADDLE

The saddle used is the saddleseat type, which sets the rider's weight back, off the horse's front quarters. A horse with less weight in the front will trot more freely. Hunt-seat saddles work poorly for this discipline because they put the rider's weight forward. You cannot ride an English horse to optimum performance if you're using a poorly made saddle or one not designed for the use you are putting it to.

Even among the saddleseat saddles, there are variations in the ways they are made, and some are better than others. Ask an experienced trainer what saddle he or she uses. It is likely that through the years the trainer will have found a brand that is durable, of good quality and well designed for riding English.

A pad should be worn beneath the saddle. Because the rider's weight is back, there is an increased chance the horse's back will become sore. A pad makes the saddle's action easier on him. Pads are specially designed to go beneath the saddle, are the same basic shape and are made of felt or a very dense black foam. Fleece pads are also available, but don't buy anything too fuzzy for show ring use. You want the pad to be inconspicuous. When you practice at home, it doesn't matter what you use as long as it is thick enough to protect the horse's back.

Cinches are made of molded rubber, patent leather or webbing. The first two are more popular in the ring.

## BITS

The English horse is shown in a double bridle, consisting of a bradoon (a type of small snaffle bit) and a curb bit (see below). Many horses work best if ridden mostly on the bradoon, but what works best varies from horse to horse. Some need more curb, or an even balance between the two bits.

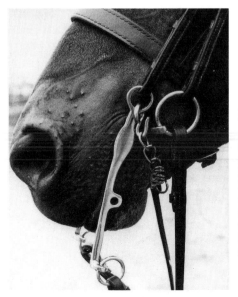

A closeup of the bits of the double bridle, the snaffle and the curb, and how they should fit. Notice the snaffle fits higher in the mouth and behind the curb chain, the heavier of the two chains seen here. The finer chain is the lip chain. Also note the position of the cavesson, the strap that circles the nose above the bits. It runs beneath all of the other straps and rests just below the tear bone.

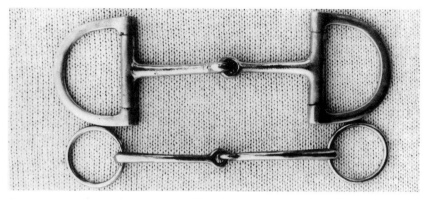

A comparison of a regular smooth snaffle, above, and a smooth bradoon.

Bits come in stainless steel or copper. Copper keeps the mouth more moist, so the bit doesn't grate across dry gums.

## SNAFFLES AND BRADOONS

Snaffles and bradoons basically are the same thing—bits with jointed mouthpieces. Bradoons are smaller and are used in double bridles (see above). When referring to a bradoon, it is equally correct to call it a snaffle.

Professionals often work the horses at home in snaffles and use the double bridle at shows. The snaffle puts pressure primarily on the corners of the mouth. It can also exert some pressure on the bars of the mouth, depending on the type of snaffle and how it is used. The action of the snaffle tends to pull the head upward and urge motion forward.

The smoother and thicker the snaffle mouthpiece, the milder it is. With some of the bits, you also can choose between mouthpieces that are straight and those that have curved sides. Snaffles with curved mouthpieces give the bit more exposure to the horse's bars, and are more severe.

Here are some of the most commonly used bradoon and snaffle mouthpieces:

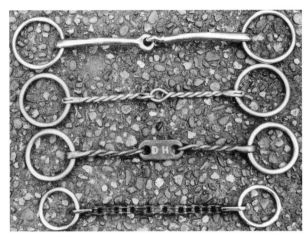

Bradoons, from the top down: the smooth, the twisted, the Dr. Bristol twisted and the bicycle chain.

Smooth        One of the mildest mouthpieces available. It usually is the first bit for young horses and can be used on veterans as well.

Twisted Wire        More severe than the smooth, this mouthpiece resembles a length of thick, twisted wire. This bit is favored for horses that are too pushy in the smooth snaffle. A double-twisted wire—a bit with two twisted wire mouthpieces in one snaffle—is also used, and is more severe than the single twist. The double-twist has a pinching effect on the tongue and corners of the mouth.

Slow Twist        A step between the smooth and twisted wire, this bit has fewer twists to the mouthpiece.

Dr. Bristol Twisted        This bit has a flat, rectangular piece of metal in the middle that divides the two twisted wire elements. It reduces the leverage of the bit on the sides of the mouth, but drops the mouthpiece down onto the bars more than bits without the divider in the middle.

Bicycle Chain        Made like the chain of a bicycle, the severity of this bit depends on what the chain looks and feels like. A thin chain with small prongs along its length can be quite severe, while a thicker chain that is smooth is less so.

# CURB BITS

The curb fits in the mouth slightly below the bradoon. It puts pressure on the tongue, bars of the mouth, under the chin and at the poll. The curb brings the nose inward. Using too much curb can encourage the horse to drop down the head and neck, causing elevation to be lost and thereby reducing the horse's action. Curb bits are used on English horses only in double bridles. The longer the shank and taller the port (the upside-down U at the center of the bit), the more severe the bit. Also, the narrower the mouthpiece, the more severe the bit, and mouthpieces wrapped in wire are more severe than those that are smooth.

Curb mouthpieces include:

Oval Port    The mildest of the mouthpieces, it is curved in a nearly crescent shape. This is a very comfortable bit, and the horse can use his tongue to move it around in his mouth without causing any problems.

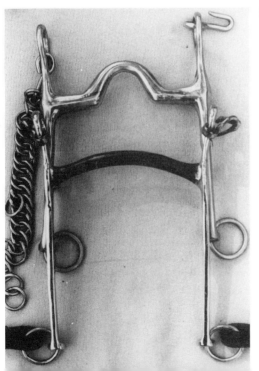

Medium port.

Medium Port      The next step up, this is a straight mouthpiece interrupted in the middle by a mild port. This bit works more on the tongue than the oval port. The wider the port, the greater the area of the tongue affected. The port also reduces the horse's ability to move the bit around with his tongue. If he lifts the bit very far, he will bring the port in contact with the roof of his mouth.

High Port      More severe than either the oval or medium port, this bit works on the roof of the mouth in addition to the tongue and the other curb pressure points. This bit emphasizes that the only comfortable head position for the horse is with the face vertical. If the head is moved out of that position, the port hits the roof of the mouth. The horse also cannot use his tongue to lift this bit off the bars without the port immediately hitting the roof of his mouth. The high port should be used only by an experienced rider with still hands who understands the effects of the bit.

Port with Rollers      Rollers are little round or oblong wheels skewered in the curve of the port (see page 55). More commonly seen in Western bits, they are used on English horses as well. The rollers turn as the horse moves his tongue back and forth beneath them. They are commonly used on the horse that tries to get his tongue over the bit or that lets his tongue hang out the side of his mouth. Their purpose is to give the horse something to do with his tongue instead.

Windsucking Bit      This odd-looking bit has a straight mouthpiece running through a metal barrel (see page 55). The barrel stretches the full length of the mouthpiece, is full of holes, and moves loosely around the mouthpiece. It is for horses that grab hold of traditional curbs and suck down air or who are irritated by the movement of a curb on their bars. With this bit, a horse can grab hold of the barrel and retain that hold, but still feel the rider's directions through the mouthpiece moving inside the barrel.

Pelham      This bit tries to combine the curb and snaffle into one bit. The mouthpiece is usually like an oval port, and attached to that is a ring on each side for a rein that acts as the snaffle rein. Also attached to the mouthpiece is a shank. A second rein attaches to the bottom of the shank to serve as the curb rein. Some riders find the Pelham easier to contend with, but it is not as functional as the combination of snaffle and curb. The bit is not held in very high regard by English trainers.

A chain under the chin is used in conjunction with all types of English curb bits. Without the chain, the curb can't work properly. The tighter the chain, the more the horse will feel the rider's hands. Beginning riders therefore should not have it too tight. More experienced riders should set the chain snug, but not to the extent that it takes great effort or pliers to latch it.

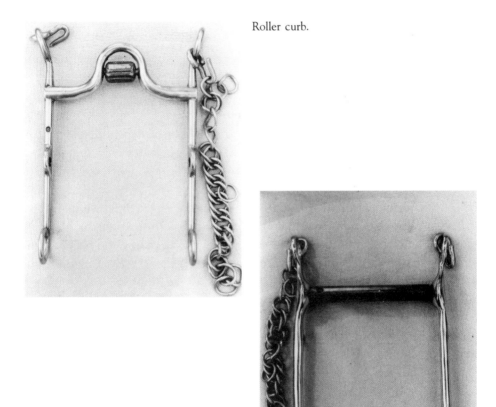

Roller curb.

Windsucking bit.

The chain attaches to the curb with curb hooks, which face outward from the horse's face. There are two kinds of hooks: the standard hook and the circular, in which the tip of the hook is bent in toward the center. Either works equally well. Standard hooks are easier to use when you're trying to attach a curb chain, an important feature if the chain is tight or your fingers are slick with horse saliva. Occasionally the snaffle will get caught on the regular hooks; circular hooks keep that from happening.

Also attaching the chain to the curb is the lip strap, which is a fine chain or leather strap running from eyelets on each side of the shank. Authorities differ on the purpose of the strap. Some contend it was originally designed to keep the curb chain in place, while others say it is to keep the horse from grabbing hold of the side of the bit with his teeth. Either way, the rules require the lip strap be used.

# MARTINGALES

Martingales cannot be used in the show ring but are frequently used in training in combination with the snaffle. The martingale adds an additional pressure point to the snaffle, shifting pressure onto the bars of the mouth, and offers leverage to bring in the nose when the horse is trying to evade the bit.

The martingale should not be used primarily to set the head, however. There is a difference between using it as a tool to set the head and using it as a backup to keep the horse from evading the bit. The head should be set by using your legs to drive the horse up to meet the bit. (How this is done will be discussed in detail in later chapters.) If you rely on the martingale instead of your legs to set the head, the head set will disappear when you remove the martingale. It's there to help you out, not to do the job that you're supposed to be doing.

The following are the most commonly used types:

Running Martingale    A strap runs from the cinch, up between the front legs, and divides in two with each ending in a ring. The device is secured with a second strap that circles the neck. The length of the martingale can be adjusted. Usually it is adjusted so that when pulled upward the rings reach at least as high as the horse's hip bones, if not higher.

More commonly seen is an adaptation of this arrangement, a training martingale, which is also called a running martingale (see below). A strap passes from the cinch up between the front legs, then divides in two with each side ending in a ring. Attached to the top of the right ring is a second strap that goes across the top of the neck to clip onto the left ring. With this martingale the rings end up more along the horse's shoulders rather than remaining more in line with the center of the horse.

Draw-rein Martingale       On each side of the horse, a rein runs from the ring at the top of the cinch, up through the snaffle and then to the rider's hands (see page 58). A variation is to run a cord from the middle of the cinch, up between the horse's legs to the snaffle, and then up to the rider's hands. An advantage of draw reins is there are no rings to adjust. In addition to the draw rein, you usually should use a direct rein, one that goes directly from the bit to your hands. Ride the horse primarily on the direct rein, using the draw rein as a backup.

German Martingale       A strap passes from the cinch, up the chest, and then divides in two. Each strap ends in a snap. The snaps pass through the snaffle rings and clip to one of a series of rings on the specially made reins (see page 58). This martingale also has a strap around the neck to hold it in place.

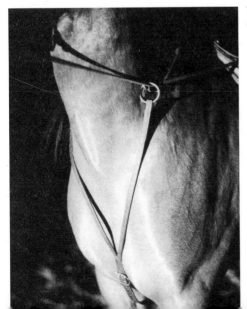

Type of running martingale most commonly used by English trainers.

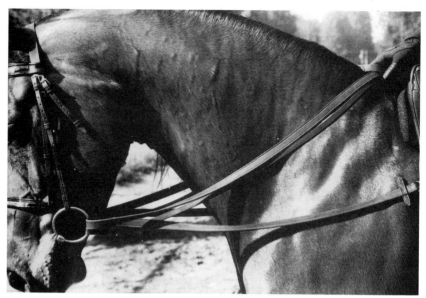

Draw reins running from the cinch to the hands. The second rein running from the bit to hands is a direct rein.

German martingale.

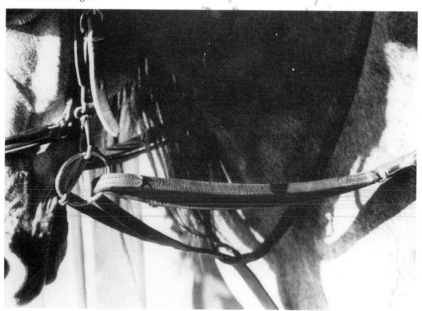

# TRAINING SHACKLES

Also called running **Ws**, shackles come in many different designs, some of which are homemade. The purpose of shackles is to encourage high knee action and help build the muscles responsible for that action. Used properly, they can be a helpful aid. Unfortunately, they are frequently abused. When overused or frequently put on too tight, they pervert the horse's motion to make it halting and unnatural. If you are not skilled in their use, it is best to avoid them entirely.

A hobble lined in sheepskin goes around each pastern. Attached to each hobble is rubber tubing. The tubing either will connect the two hobbles or run from each hobble up to the cinch. Another version of training shackles has bootlike devices that go over the hoofs. Elastic runs up from the shackles to a leather strap over the horse's back.

The tubing or elastic should be tight enough to offer resistance when the horse moves, but not so tight that his movement is labored. Shackles that are too tight make the horse look like he is moving in slow motion, and they can cause pulled muscles and other injuries.

# ACTION RINGS, CHAINS AND RATTLERS

Some trainers use action rings, chains and rattlers to make a horse trot higher or to get a horse that is lazy with his hocks to use them better. Such devices are illegal in the ring.

Action rings are made of rolled or stitched leather and are usually fairly light. Action chains are either single or double strands (see page 60) or are covered by rubber tubing. Rattlers are aluminum or wood beads threaded on a leather or chain ring. If you feel it would be beneficial to use an action ring or chain, take care to select one that is not so heavy that it will be painful to your horse (see page 60).

Also included in the class of action devices are weighted bell boots. The weight encourages a high trot. If properly adjusted, they should not move around on the pastern to the extent that they cause pain. Of the action-producing devices discussed, the light chains and weighted

Light motion chain.

Heavy motion chain. A chain
this large is likely to be painful to
the horse.

bell boots are the most popular. There is something of a stigma attached to the use of these devices, since the Arabian horse is supposed to be displaying "natural" talent in English classes, but I suspect the use of these devices is fairly common.

As with the shackles, you should not use any of the various action devices unless you know how to use them, how much to use them, why you are using them (because everyone else does is not a valid reason) and how they will affect the horse. All the devices on the market are not going to make an iffy horse a national contender. You should also not put a talented horse at risk by using something that he probably doesn't need, and that you do not know how to use properly.

# SWEATS

A sweat does just that—makes the horse sweat. Most commonly seen are plastic or rubbery coverings wrapped around the horse's neck, but sweats can also be used to cover most of the body. The intent is to reduce the size of the neck or body by sweating inches off while the horse exercises. Since the inches removed are water, they don't stay off, but if you use the sweats properly you can keep the inches off long enough to get through a show. Various concoctions such as a solution of glycerine and alcohol are used beneath the sweats to make the horse sweat more.

Some horses also wear neck wraps, also called collars, made of fleece or sheepskin. These are worn every day in the stall to try to retain the slimness achieved by sweating the neck. Their effectiveness is questionable—even the people who use them don't know if they work.

If you're going to sweat a horse's neck, don't try to do it when you're riding the horse. If you put a sweat on his neck, then ask him to set his head, he has to nearly strangle himself to comply. I don't know how many English horses I've seen wearing neck sweats and wheezing around the practice arena. The horse will learn that setting the head is uncomfortable and will become increasingly reluctant to do it even without the sweat.

# 6

# Starting the Horse

THE ENGLISH HORSE IS STARTED late in his second year or as a three-year-old. When training begins and how quickly it progresses depends entirely on the horse. He will tell you what he is ready for, and when. Horses are individuals and can't be made to conform to set training formulas.

Here, we'll consider "starting" to mean when you begin preparations to long-line the horse. Prior to long lining, the horse should lunge easily in both directions, respond to voice commands while on the line and move away from the whip.

## LONG LINING

Long lining also is called ground driving or long reining. It is used to start a young horse and continues to be used throughout the horse's career. It offers the veteran horse variety to keep him sharp and gives the handler the opportunity to work the horse and see the overall picture the horse is presenting.

For the green horse, the best place to long-line is in a small round bullpen. One that is approximately thirty feet around works well. The shape and size of the enclosure will make your job easier. In an enclosed area, the horse also cannot get away from you.

In lungeing and the beginning of long lining, voice commands are necessary; except for the line and the whip, you have no other means of communicating with the horse. Voice cues should be kept simple. Frequently used are "Whoa" to stop; "Walk" to walk; a clucking sound to boost a walking horse into a trot or to demand more effort from a horse that is trotting; a kissing sound to initiate a canter; and "whoop," to drop the horse down one gait, such as from a canter to a trot. Voice cues can vary from handler to handler. Some use "whoop" as a cue to slow down. It's not necessary to use any of these sounds more than one or twice in succession. For example, a horse will ignore the clucking sound if it is used too much.

Later in the horse's training, most of these voice cues will fall by the wayside. With a ridden horse, the only voice cues to survive usually are the cluck, "whoop," and occasionally "Whoa."

The horse will be introduced to the long-line equipment piece by piece, with the surcingle coming first. The surcingle goes on like a cinch and buckles on the left side of the horse. It fits just snug enough so that it won't slide around on the horse's back. After you put the surcingle on the horse, let him carry it during his usual lungeing routine until he becomes accustomed to the way it feels. Some horses find the surcingle no big deal and carry it well within a week. Others are alarmed by the snug strap around their bellies and can take considerably longer to get used to it.

Once the horse is lungeing well in the surcingle, add a crupper and continue his usual lungeing routine until he wears it easily, without bucking, scooting his rump or tucking his tail. The crupper runs from the surcingle and loops back beneath the tail. Tighten just enough so it does not move around, otherwise the horse will object if it is too tight.

Next, add a bridle with a smooth snaffle bit and no reins. Put the halter over the top of the bridle, and lunge the horse with the line attached to the halter.

After the horse is carrying the complete rig without distress, add the long lines (see below). Run the lines to the bit through the surcingle rings that best match the level where the horse carries his head (see page 65). As he becomes more experienced, thread the lines through progressively higher rings. Through the lines, maintain light contact with the horse's mouth. This is a light hold, not a pull. Pulling on a horse encourages him to push back, exactly what you don't want him to do. Think of your arms as if they were attached to gears that can only be brought in and let out a notch at a time. A light hold is in one notch. You pull to get to the notch, then click into the notch and maintain the hold instead of maintaining the pull. A moderate hold is a notch tighter that you can click into and maintain. A strong hold is in a few notches more.

This doesn't mean that your hands just "freeze" or that movements are jerky—there is a great deal of give and take, but not by pulling. You give a notch, take a notch, give two. Urge the horse forward with

Canadian Love in the long lines, showing good elevation at the walk. Begin working the horse in the long lines at the walk in an enclosed area. Try a few turns to get him used to the lines. When the horse is responding well, move on to faster gaits. Photograph by Chick Stoll.

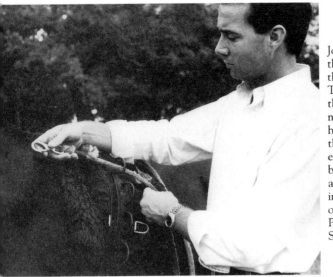

John Rannenberg threading the long lines through the surcingle. Thread the lines through the ring that best matches the level the horse carries his head. As the horse becomes more experienced, he will become more elevated, and you can use increasingly higher rings on the surcingle. Photograph by Chick Stoll.

John Rannenberg working Canadian Love at the walk. Photograph by Chick Stoll.

voice and lightly tap the whip on his rump if necessary.

For the first outing, don't try to get too fancy. Work the horse first at a walk, allowing him to get used to having the lines attached (see above). Try a few turns into the wall. Those are the easiest to begin with, since the wall or fence is there to guide him around. To turn him, take a stronger hold on his outside line and give with the inside line. If he is responding calmly to the presence of the lines, work him both ways at the trot and canter as well.

As he progresses in his lessons, you can ask him to perform turns away from the wall, do serpentines and flex from side to side. Asking the horse to flex his head from side to side is a good way to warm him up at the beginning of a lesson. It gives him time to focus his mind on work and makes him more supple and responsive.

Your primary goals are to teach him to move forward and respect and give to the bit. Those are the same principles you will continue to reinforce throughout his performance career. The two are also interconnected. A horse that is not going forward will lag behind the bit, or hold it rigidly. A horse that leans on the bit is not balanced or moving forward properly.

A horse does not achieve forward motion just by moving forward. A horse can be cantering without having forward motion. Forget the standard dictionary definition of "forward." In training terms, forward motion means the horse is driving his body forward with his hocks working strongly and well beneath him. The motion generated propels his whole body forward, allowing him to balance himself and shift weight off his front quarters to achieve elevation. He is collected and able to respond quickly to the demands of the rider or handler. A horse that is not moving forward flails out behind himself with his hocks, not generating any more propulsion than it takes to cover the ground. He is incapable of shifting the weight off his front quarters, because there is not enough support behind to allow him to do so. He has difficulty responding to the rider or handler in a coordinated manner.

Forward motion is promoted by the way in which you use your hands and legs—or, in the case of long lining, hands, voice, whip and where you position yourself. The hands create a barrier that tells the horse his face is not to move beyond a certain position. Don't pull. Take a light hold and maintain it. Take more of a hold on the inside rein than on the outside to keep him moving bent with the circle. Green horses tend to want to bend the other way.

You can encourage him to move forward to the barrier set by the hands by using your voice cues, tapping him lightly on the rump with the whip, and by positioning yourself even with his hip. You are, in a sense, gently chasing him forward, just as he might be chased by the dominant horse in a herd. The dominant horse would follow behind, nipping at his rump. You will stay toward his rear as well.

If you stand too far toward the front of the horse when trying to drive him forward, he may perceive that you are about to cut him off or block his path. Horses are more easily driven forward from behind. Give a voice command, such as a cluck, to tell him to move forward. Cluck once. If he does not respond promptly or is lazy about it, tap him with the whip. Be consistent. You want him to understand what is expected when he hears that sound. The cluck means move up, *right now.*

When the horse recognizes the barrier set by your hands and his head gives to the bit, even a little, give him some slack as a reward. If you immediately take up what he has given you, all he learns is that it doesn't matter if he gives to the bit or not. You must be consistent, and give every time he does. When he is quite green, the slack you give him should be at least a few inches. When working a seasoned horse, the amount you give becomes more subtle, perhaps just relaxing your fingers. Giving teaches the horse to yield to the bit, even as he moves forward to it. He will begin looking for your guidance as to where his head should be.

Giving to him at the appropriate time also includes the cues you are using to drive him forward. If he gives to you and moves forward, stop cueing. He's already done what you asked for.

What about the opposite of giving? The green horse gives to you, you give to him, then he ungratefully tries to root out his nose and loose collection. It can all take place in a matter of a few strides. When he starts to fall apart, your first desire will be to pull his face back in, but that's not what the horse needs you to do. Instead, regain the light hold you had, and drive him forward to the bit from behind with your voice and whip. When he gives, give to him again. Gradually he will maintain the proper position and forward motion for longer periods of time. Don't worry too much at first about trying to set his head high. Find a position that is comfortable for him, and teach him to give to the bit and move forward before you teach elevation.

As he progresses, he will be able to give you stronger forward motion, more elevation, a better set to the head (see page 68). Again, all of these come from driving the horse forward to meet the barrier set by the reins. It takes consistency and routine. When the horse is responding easily, driving forward well and elevating, you can add a side check or overcheck (see page 69). These are straps that run from the top ring of the surcingle, up the neck, and down through the bridle to the bit. They are adjusted to pull the head upward, encouraging more elevation (see page 69). However, they should not be attached until the long-line horse has been warmed up and is ready to elevate.

In working the horse, don't rush. A confused, frustrated or angry horse won't focus on what you are trying to teach him. Try to accept that at first he is not going to look much like the English horse of your dreams. Just keep that picture in your mind, and work slowly toward it.

Workouts should be brief for young horses. Their attention spans are limited, and you want them to find the work enjoyable, interesting and challenging. Fifteen minutes is adequate for a young horse that is progressing well, and around twenty to thirty minutes of vigorous work for a more experienced horse is desirable. If the lesson isn't going well, work until you get something accomplished, then put the horse away as a reward. Regardless of the type of workout, whether it is long lining or under saddle, always finish on a positive note. The young horse should be worked five to six days a week. The veteran does not need to work as often, but even if not ridden or long lined, still needs frequent exercise.

John Rannenberg working Canadian Love in the long lines at the trot. Photograph by Chick Stoll.

John Rannenberg connecting the overcheck, which is used to help the horse elevate. It is used only on advanced horses. Photograph by Chick Stoll.

A closeup of Canadian Love wearing the overcheck and bridle. The tightness of the overcheck varies but usually is adjusted tight enough to pull the horse's head upward, while still allowing him to tuck in his nose. Photograph by Chick Stoll.

# BREAKING

After three to four months of long lining, the horse will know most of the principles he needs to be ridden. After so much preparation, having you on his back will not present many surprises for him—or you either, for that matter. A few days before the first ride, put the saddle and bridle on the horse and lunge him. Lunge him tacked every day until he's carrying it well. It should not take long.

For the first rides, use a small enclosed area like a bullpen. Lunge the horse tacked as you did the day before. This time you will add a martingale. You may want to put it on after lungeing, or secure it to the saddle so that if the horse sticks his head down while on the line the martingale will not slide up his neck (see below). After he's warmed up and is done playing on the line, you can get on. Start out slow, walking around the pen and doing a few large circles so he can get used to your weight.

John Rannenberg adjusting Canadian Love's bridle. Photograph by Chick Stoll.

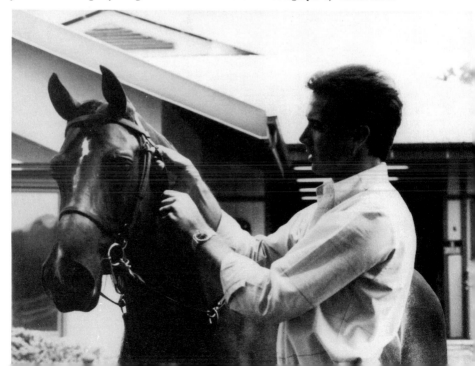

If you know the horse well, you probably will be able to predict with a fair amount of accuracy how he will respond to your first ride. He will undoubtedly respond to it the same way he did with other experiences.

How much you will ask of him on that first ride depends on him. If in his first lesson he finds a rider on his back truly alarming or if he acts like your weight might topple him at any moment, take it slow. Just walk for your first few lessons, and save the faster gaits for later. On the other hand, if on your first outing he's taking it well and seems to be handling your weight adequately, go ahead and trot and canter. Since the two of you have done your homework, he should understand most of what you want. It is all right to lean forward a bit when asking him to pick up a faster gait if it seems to help him to move forward. Later, you will help him best by shifting your weight back.

On his back you do much the same as you did with the long lines—take hold of the reins with your hands, and push him to it with your legs. The hold should be uneven. An equal hold on both reins it gives him a surface to lean on. In general have a slightly stronger hold on the inside rein. Don't expect too much of him at first. The addition of your weight has thrown him way off balance and popped his nose out. He understands what you are doing with your hands, but since this is his first experience with leg pressure, it is all rather confusing to him.

Through his earlier long-line lessons he learned to move away from pressure. Now you will teach him that that principle applies to leg pressure, too. The way you use your legs is the same as for a veteran horse, but as with all your movements, everything is stronger and more exaggerated. Use the same technique every time. Consistency is very important to his understanding and responding. The green horse will also have an easier time of it if only one person rides him. Different riders will feel different to him, just as different horses feel different to you. A certain amount of consistency is lost when riders are switched.

In teaching the horse about leg pressure, keep your legs back around the cinch area, and use them only when you want something from him (see page 72). If you are squeezing and kicking all the time, you are practically begging him to ignore you. Spurs should not be used on a green horse. The reason he feels unresponsive is that you have not taught him yet what responsive means. If you need to use a whip, use it on the shoulder or behind your leg as a reinforcement of the leg cue. One or two light taps usually is plenty.

Riding instructors refer to the proper way to use your legs as "squeezing." The term is deceptive, because it makes it sound like you clamp on to the horse with the calves of your legs and squeeze with all your might as the horse moves along. A horse quickly learns to ignore that kind of squeezing. A squeeze is not that constant. It is more of a bump timed with the horse's strides. Your leg comes in, meets the horse's side, presses into the side, then releases. The squeeze usually only lasts the time it takes the horse to complete one stride, but can last for a number of strides, depending upon the gait and what you are trying to accomplish. With the green horse, you may be kicking more than squeezing, but as he progresses he will respond to increasingly subtle cues.

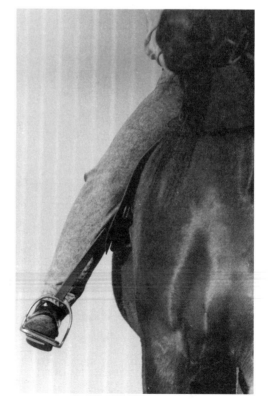

Good leg position for when not cueing the horse. When a cue is given, the calves come in to the horse's sides. Some riders hold their legs closer in to the horse than this, and others hold them farther away. In English Pleasure, do whatever works best for you. Photograph by Greg Lehman.

To cue him and help him find balance, you will use your hands, legs and weight in the following ways:

Walk      Put your weight in the center of the horse and offer support with your hands. If he is dawdling along, your first impulse will be to feed him rein. Instead, keep contact with his mouth. He needs the support that gives him and guidance about where he should be positioning himself. As you maintain contact, push him forward with your legs—but not constantly. Bump him forward, then take your legs off. Then, when he slackens, bump him again. A green horse tends to wander. Your goal is to encourage him to move forward without wandering. If you want a straight line and he begins to fade left, you will bump him back in line with your right leg. You may or may not need a little left rein.

Trot      Again, you will support him with your hands instead of throwing him loose rein when you ask him to trot. Shorten your reins or set your hands farther back than at the walk, then give him a cluck and bring both legs into his sides. Leaning forward may help him at first. Later on, leaning back will be more beneficial. As soon as he trots, stop squeezing, and resume squeezing only when you need to drive him forward. The squeezes will be timed with your posting, with your legs coming in for the squeeze as you sit down, and coming off as you rise up.

His trot is going to be pretty dismal. Don't worry about it. When his balance returns and he gets stronger, if he has the talent, the trot will be there.

Canter      Pull his head slightly to the outside of the circle, shift your weight to the outside and kick with only the outside leg. The principle is to get weight off the inside, helping him pick the proper lead. Some trainers tip the head to the inside of the circle instead, then cue with the outside leg. Both ways work. Pick whichever you prefer, then use it consistently. If you have taught him a verbal cue for canter, use it. He will trot a little before plunging into a canter. That's fine. Once he canters, stop kicking, shift your weight to the middle and straighten and support his head. When he begins picking up the leads well, you no longer will need to pull his head to the side or give the verbal cue. Just shift your weight and give the leg cue.

Help him along with squeezes of your legs when he needs them. The canter likely will be quite fast at first. He's off balance, tense and uncollected. It is easier for him to go fast than slow.

You probably will want to shift your weight backward, stiffen your back, push your feet forward and pull back on the reins. That's not going to impress the horse much. After all, he weighs a thousand pounds and you're pulling on him with two little leather straps. You have given up all of your controls except your hands, and at the same time you have given the horse pressure to lean into.

Stay relaxed, and let your relaxation seep into him. Keep your weight toward the center and your back supple. Tilt your pelvis slightly forward and imagine that you are sending your weight down through your body and into his. Your legs maintain their position, so you are not standing in the stirrups or curling your legs around the horse's belly. Instead of pulling hard on the reins, take hold for a few strides, then relax, then hold and relax again.

At the same time, push him forward lightly with your legs, squeezing and releasing. It may not sound like a very sane thing to do to a horse that is already moving way too fast, but believe it or not, using legs slows the horse down. He is moving too fast because he is tense, uncollected and unbalanced. By working with your weight, hands and legs, you are helping him to regain his balance, relax, and work toward collection so he can slow down. This does not happen instantly. You may have a number of lessons with the wind whipping by your ears before he begins rating back consistently. Regulation of speed is always something you work on, even with more experienced horses.

Circle        Bring the horse's head to the inside of the circle, drop your weight to the inside stirrup (your upper body remains straight) and squeeze with your outside leg (see page 75). As he moves into the circle, use the inside leg to bend his body to the shape of the circle. Occasionally use an outside leg and outside rein to keep him from overbending. The faster the gait, the larger the circle you should make with the green horse. He does not have the balance yet to maintain the gait in small circles.

To circle the horse, bring his head to the inside of the circle, drop your weight to the inside stirrup and squeeze with the outside leg.

Corners     The corners in an arena offer the greatest opportunity for the horse to lose all the balance and collection you helped him achieve on the straightaway. The proper position for the horse to take a corner is with body bending around the curve, with the rump following the path traveled by the front quarters (see page 76.) Green horses, and even experienced horses, may try to go around the corner like their vertebrae have suddenly fused together and they cannot bend. They crook their heads to the outside and go around with their shoulders leading the way. Or they will bend their heads to the inside but drop the rest of their bodies outside the curve of the corner.

Either way, the horse is not bending his body. The hindquarters that should be driving the horse forward instead drop out of alignment. The horse loses impulsion, and then collection. Consequently you spend the pass down the rail trying to get the horse collected and moving forward again, then lose it in the next corner, get it back, and lose it again. In a class, falling apart in the corners can cost you dearly.

To keep the horse together through the corners, use a combination of hand and leg. Prepare the horse to take the corner even before the curve begins. Bring the horse back a little. You want to increase collection, but not speed. The green horse will not respond completely, but give the command anyway. He will pick it up in time.

As the curve of the corner begins, take more hold of the inside rein than the outside, give a little with the outside rein and squeeze the horse with your inside leg to bend his body to the curve of the corner (see below). Keep the horse from bending too far by occasionally using the outside rein and the outside leg. How much rein and leg to use, which ones, and how often, depends on the horse. A green horse is going to need a lot more leg and rein than a veteran.

The position of the horse's body, as seen from above, when turning a corner. The spine should follow the shape of the corner.

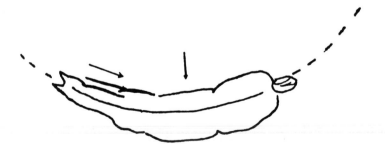

Help the horse conform to the curve by using the inside rein and the inside leg.

Keep your weight in the center of the horse throughout the curve. Leaning into circles is for barrel racing. You also want to watch how deep you are asking the horse to go into the corner. The faster the gait, the more difficult it is for the horse to go deep. An experienced horse can handle it with a little help from the rider. A green horse may break gait.

As the horse exits the corner, straighten his head, and squeeze with both legs to move him down the wall. On the way around the ring, you occasionally will use one rein or the other to make an adjustment in his position.

Moving On and Off the Rail      Shift your weight to the inside stirrup, and push with your outside leg until the horse moves away from the rail. You can take a little more hold on the inside rein to encourage him to move in that direction, but not so much that he begins to turn. Move back to the rail by shifting your weight to the outside stirrup and pressing with the inside leg.

Downward Transitions      To move from the canter to the trot, take a slightly stronger hold on the reins, say "Whoop" and drop your weight down into the horse's back. The weight feels like what is used to slow the horse, only it is more exaggerated. Your stomach muscles contract and the lower spine curls and pushes weight downward as if you are tying to drop through him to the ground under his belly. As the horse breaks into a trot, bring your legs into his sides and cluck once. Begin posting, using your weight to encourage him forward. As was said earlier, in the beginning stages of training, this may mean putting your weight forward.

During the brief moment during the post when your buttocks are in contact with his back, drive him forward with your buttocks. Instead of just plopping down on his back, come down lightly, pushing your seat bones down and forward, angling toward his front quarters instead of straight down.

As the horse moves forward to your hands and collects, give him back the light hold you had prior to the transition. At the trot, your reins will be a little shorter than at the walk.

To move from a canter or trot to a walk or stop, take moderate hold of the reins (don't pull, just set your hands back farther than they were) and drive your weight down. As the horse reaches the end of the transition, put your legs lightly on his sides. If you don't use any leg during the transition, the horse will come down on his front quarters instead of his hindquarters as he should. He also may drop behind the bridle.

To an observer, the horse coming down on his front quarters looks like he is about to stumble. He loses elevation and balance, and tends to thrust out his face. Instead, you want to push him to the bridle so he comes down in a balanced manner.

The horse knows what gait to break down to by the cue you give him and how long it lasts. If you are going from a canter to a trot, he will learn that as he reaches the trot he'll hear a cluck and you'll start driving him forward if you want him to trot. If he's going down to a walk, he will pass through a few steps of the trot without getting a trot cue. Instead, he will continue receiving the cue telling him to drop down another gait. As he drops into the walk, if you want him to continue walking, stop driving your weight downward and squeeze him forward. Don't cluck. That means trot.

If you want him to stop, continue the downward weight. As he begins to stop, use a little leg to push him to the bit. Stopping is a forward movement. When he stops and gives to the bit, give rein back to him, and take your legs off his sides.

Backing     Take a moderate hold on the reins (don't pull), and apply a little leg. The legs tell the horse he has to do something, but the hands are saying the horse cannot go forward. The hold is stronger than it would have been had you asked the horse to walk forward. You have in essence shut a door in front of the horse. The only place left to go is back. If the first time you do this, he takes one step back, that's a good start. Give to him, tell him he's a good horse and move on to something else. Don't overwork on backing. A few times per session is plenty.

The focus of the exercise is not just to teach him to walk backward on command, you also want him to give to the bit and come up off it. Poking out the nose and shuffling backwards is not acceptable. When he understands the basics about moving backwards, back him until he softens on the bridle, then give to him, walk him forward and move on to something else for a while.

# 7

# Practice and Tuning

THE DOUBLE BRIDLE IS INTRODUCED into the training program in the fourth or fifth month. That's a lot of hardware to be putting into the horse's mouth, and he has to be ready. The double bridle is not going to "fix" problems the horse is having in the snaffle. In fact some problems will be made worse, for example, if the horse is still afraid of the bit.

Before using the double bridle, the horse should be working well in the snaffle and be responsive to it. He may backslide somewhat when you first begin using the double bridle because the leverage action of the curb will be new to him.

Your use of the curb should be very light at first. If you grab hold of it and jerk his face in with brute force on his first outing, you are telling him that he had a right to be worried about the curb. A stressed horse creates problems in order to deal with the problem he is having with you. He may bob his head around behind the bit or stick out his tongue. He can think up behaviors you may never get rid of.

Use a light touch, and let the horse get use to the curb. Select a curb that is mild—thick, with a low port and moderate shanks. If your hands move much when you ride, keep in mind that the horse feels every bump. A mild bit will minimize your battery of his mouth. A young horse should still have a good mouth and not need a severe bit. Work him in the double bridle as you did in the snaffle until he accepts the bridle well, and is moving forward without sinking back off the bit or stiffening against it.

After the double bridle becomes standard fare for the horse, you probably will want to go back to using the snaffle during practice. Most trainers prefer to work in the snaffle.

# WORKOUT ROUTINES

You can add variety to the horse's workouts by riding him with other horses, and outside of the arena. Riding him when other horses are in the ring is good preparation for the show ring. Some horses get distracted or rattled by horses that pass close by them or bump into them. Some are timid and lack confidence. The company of other horses will improve your horse's attitude and ability to work despite distractions, as will riding him outside the arena.

The round-and-round pattern of the ring can get dull both for you and the horse. Going out freshens the mind and keeps the horse bright and looking for what comes next. Dealing with experiences outside will build his confidence. If he manages to make it by a scary bush or over a bank, he'll begin to believe he's a pretty brave horse. His attitude affects how he looks. Cocky looks much better than timid. When it's show time, confidence will make him bolder, a valuable commodity in an English horse. He will push through a dense pack of horses without hesitation.

If you have nowhere to ride outside the arena, do the best you can to give the horse some variety. Before you begin, put a coat over the rail one day or throw down a few paper plates—nothing that will cause alarm but enough to keep the horse looking for new things. At the same time, you do not want to carry this to extremes and have him become indifferent to everything. If you try to scare the daylights out of him all the time, eventually nothing will impress him. Some people use fire extinguishers and firecrackers to get the horse elevated and his ears up. If it takes that much, your horse may look pretty bored in the ring.

Before moving into a heavy workout always give the horse a chance to warm up physically and mentally. Blood moves into the muscles and his attention moves toward to you. Horses want to start a workout differently. Some prefer a nice rolling canter, others a moderate trot. After you've ridden your horse for a while, you will be able to tell his preference. A few exercises, to be discussed shortly, will get him thinking about work.

Lungeing the horse before riding usually is not necessary once he gains a little experience under saddle. The exception is a cold-backed horse—one that bucks or humps his back during the early part of the workout. And some horses simply work better if lunged first. For example, WN Astra, the 1990 English Pleasure Scottsdale champion, is brighter and more willing to work if he gets to romp and play on the lunge line first. Without lunge-line work, he tends to be sulky and it takes longer to get him to begin working well under saddle. If you have one of these horses, or it just makes you feel better to lunge the horse first, go ahead.

During the workout under saddle, give attention to all of the gaits, including the walk. The walk often is neglected in English horses. When they get in the ring, many creep along like they have just been inflicted with arthritis. They are just waiting to launch into another gait, rather than concentrating on the walk. Some horses that look great at the trot and canter lose their composure at the walk. As long as judges are asking for the walk, the horse needs to be schooled at the walk. The horse should appear collected and be moving forward briskly.

At the normal trot, the horse should be moving forward, collected and showing moderate speed. Some people also work the horse in a slower, collected trot that the rider can sit. Although it is not used in English classes, this can be helpful in training. The third trot used is the extended trot. This is a fairly advanced gait that is called for in some classes. The extremely green horse usually does not have the muscle development or level of skill to do it well. Later in training, when he can collect and elevate more strongly, he will be able to perform it better.

The canter is collected and has moderate speed (see below). The hand gallop shows a longer stride, and because of that usually is faster, but the speed should not be extreme. The horse's head should remain steady and not bob or weave at any of the gaits.

When practicing for the show ring, go through all of the things you will be asked for in the ring. (The gaits requested in various English

Canadian Love showing good form at the canter under the guidance of John Rannenberg. Photograph by Chick Stoll.

classes are detailed in Chapter 1.) Demand from the horse that he give you the best he can that day. Make allowances if he's experiencing an off day—horses have bad days too. At the show, you will push for optimum performance every minute he is in the ring. You won't get it if you don't ask him for effort at home. He does not have to be perfect, but he does have to try hard. That is why twenty to thirty minutes constitutes a good workout time. During those minutes, he should really be working.

During the sessions you can use a number of exercises to increase his responsiveness, make him more supple, and focus his mind. Exercises will offer variety to the lesson as well. While some exercises involve skills you will use in the ring, some are done just for the good effects they have on the horse. Do some exercises at the beginning, and add others throughout. Devise a program of exercise that seems to work best for your horse. In general, the exercises are a good way to help your horse warm up and start thinking about work. However, horses that are somewhat wound up tend to benefit more from the exercises done in the middle of the workout—after they are less edgy and are paying attention. Exercises include:

Circles     At either direction, circle at the walk, trot or canter, bending the horse's body to the curve of the circle. This is a good exercise for a horse at any level.

Figure Eight     This is two circles, one ridden clockwise and the other counterclockwise, that are joined. If done at the canter, the horse changes lead in the middle where the circles are joined. The horse does a simple change, dropping down to a trot in the middle, then picks up the appropriate lead.

Bending the Neck to the Side     This can be done at a standstill or while moving. To do it at a standstill, halt the horse, then bring one hand back and give with the other so the horse's head comes around toward your boot (see page 85). Set your hand so he receives slack when his head is where you want it and bumps the bit when he tries to withdraw. Don't try to hold his head where you want

83

it. He can hold his own head. When he catches on to what you want, he will leave the head turned on a slack rein until you tug the other side and tell him to straighten. Do this to both the left and right side. This is a good exercise for a horse at any level.

To do the exercise on the move, bring your inside hand back, give with the outside hand, and put your inside leg against his side. Keep your weight in the center of his body or slightly to the outside. The cues you give are asking him to walk straight down the rail, while keeping his head to the inside. Your weight and inside leg keep him from turning in a circle. Instead of asking the horse to bend to one side for a few moments, then to the other, you will ask the horse to bend only to the inside. You can work the other side when you reverse.

Teach this first at the walk, then at the trot and canter. This is a good exercise for horses at all levels but the very green. But remember that the faster the gait, the harder it is for him. How much you ask for and at what pace depends on the horse's abilities. A more agile, supple horse will have an easier time of it and can give you more. A young, leggy horse that still is having trouble keeping track of what his body is doing will have some difficulty with this exercise. It still is a good exercise for him. Just don't ask for quite so much.

Moving On and Off the Rail        Move the horse off the wall with your outside leg and back on with the inside leg, shifting your weight away from the leg you are using. Use this exercise for any level of horse.

Side Passing        Some trainers use this as an exercise to get the horse listening to the legs. The ability to sidepass also is the result of a horse's having learned to respect and move away from leg pressure. It is a sign that he understands leg pressure and is paying attention. If you got on a veteran show horse that had never been asked to side pass, and gave him the appropriate cues, chances are he would side pass. He might not do it well, but he probably would give it a try because he understands he is to move away from leg pressure and respect the bit.

As an exercise, it is used with intermediate and advanced horses that have an understanding of leg pressure. The cues for side passing are reminiscent of those used for backing. Your hands tell the horse he

One exercise to help supple the neck and increase response to the bit is to bring the horse's head to your leg. Photograph by Chick Stoll.

cannot go forward, while at the same time your leg says he has to move. Shift your weight to one side and squeeze with the leg on that side. At the same time, take a moderate hold on the reins to keep him from moving forward. If at first he takes only a step or two, that's fine. Move on to something else and come back to it later.

Turn on the Forehand     This is another tuning exercise for a horse that understands leg pressure well. The point is to make him more responsive yet. Standing still, bend the horse's head to the side. While your hold is stronger on the side to which the head is bent, you also have contact with the other side. Move your leg on the bent side back slightly, and squeeze with that leg only. Your weight is in the center of the horse. The horse should move his hindquarters around the front, taking few to no steps with the front pivot leg. Start out with a few steps, and work up to where he can go completely around.

Turn on the Haunches     This is like the above move, only you turn the horse on his hindquarters instead of the front. It is for responsiveness tuning in the horse that understands leg pressure. Bend the horse's neck slightly to the side. Shift your weight to that side, then squeeze with the opposite leg. The horse should move his front quarters around the hind, with few to no steps taken on the hind leg he pivots around. Start out with just a step or two, and work up to where he can go completely around.

# BITTING

Bitting up a horse for a short period of time before or during the workout is helpful to getting the horse to soften off of the bridle. To bit the horse, either tie the reins back behind the saddle, or run them beneath the stirrup leathers and tie them on top of the saddle (see page 87). How tight they should be is dictated by the stage of the horse's training. Bit a young inexperienced horse fairly loosely. His nose should be tipped in to the point that he feels solid pressure if he tries to put his nose out very far. At the same time, if he moves his nose in away from the pressure, there should be enough slack to allow him to feel an immediate reward. If it's so tight he can't find an immediate release from the pressure, he may panic and struggle against the bit or throw himself over backwards.

If you go at it gradually and keep the build and abilities of the horse in mind, you should not have any problems. Start out by bitting him loosely. When he is handling that easily, you can bit him progressively tighter over time until you can bit the head in the position that you would want it to be in for the show ring (see page 87). The reins should be slightly uneven so he does not have as much to push against. At its tightest, the reins still should never be so tight that the horse is physically unable to come off the bit. A horse with a thicker neck has to be bitted more loosely than one with a thin, well-shaped neck.

You can bit the horse either with its head in the center or bent to the side. Like bitting to the center, bitting the horse to the side also is a gradual process. Bit him progressively tighter over time until he is bent to the degree you want.

Bitting is just another way for the horse to learn to give to the bit. If during a workout he's getting pushy or is not responding to the bit as well as you would like, you can get off, bit him up and let him work against himself for a while. You can bit him standing still (in the arena or even in his stall prior to the workout), lunge him bitted, or bit him

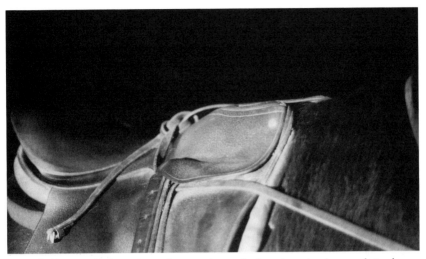

When bitting up the horse, run the reins beneath the stirrup leathers and tie them on top of the saddle, as shown here.

John Rannenberg bitting up Canadian Love. Bit the horse so that his nose is brought in, while still allowing the horse to give to the bit, relieving the pressure of the reins on his mouth. Photograph by Chick Stoll.

and work him free of the line. A horse bitted for work on the move is bitted so his face is overtucked (face is inside vertical) when he is standing still. When he moves, forward impulsion and elevation give him more slack in the rein. The result is a vertical headset. His nose may even be out a little.

Working the bitted horse on the move is helpful for a horse that is not moving forward consistently in the bridle. On the ground, you can urge him forward with voice and whip, and see what he is doing.

Bitting to the side, which is preferable to bitting the horse straight, helps supple his body as well as making him give to the bit. It also is a good technique to use on a horse that is more sluggish to respond on one side than the other, or feels stiffer on one side. It is fairly common for a horse to go slightly better one way rather than the other. Like right-handed and left-handed people, horses have dominant sides, too. You can help him work better on his problem side by bitting him toward that side, either standing still or moving. Moving, he is to circle around you in the normal fashion of a lunged horse, his head bent to the inside, and not spinning around in tiny circles. Keep him in the circle by urging him forward with whip and voice.

The amount of time he spends bitted should be fairly brief. Ten to fifteen minutes is plenty.

# ELEVATION

Elevation is vital to the English horse. A horse that does not elevate cannot trot to his best ability because the weight of his front quarters gets in the way.

For the rider, attaining that elevation is a matter of technique and timing. A professional trainer riding can make the horse look considerably taller, and trot higher than an amateur rider can. For a lesson in the effects of elevation, go out to the warmup arena at a show and watch preparations for an amateur class. If it is a fairly large or prestigious show, you'll see a group of amateurs standing in the middle of the ring watching their horses go around with trainers on them. Watch how the horses go with the trainers on them, then watch the horses go with the amateurs on them, then watch the horses in the class.

Depending on the skill of the amateur, this is what you will see:

With the professional up, the horse will look bigger and bolder and will trot higher. With the amateur up, the horse will retain that look for a while, but then will deflate like a balloon with a slow leak. If the amateur is quite good, the deflation is slight. If he or she is not, you will see quite a difference. The "coating" left on the horse by the trainer is wearing off. The elevation begins to fade, the neck drops an inch or two, the trot is not as high, the canter not as buoyant, and the nose may poke out slightly. The deflation tends to be more pronounced in the ring because the trainer cannot stand out in the middle and yell, "You're losing him! Right rein, right leg!" At the Nationals, it is fairly common for the trainer to remain on the horse until just before the gate opens for the amateur class.

The loss of elevation is the result of other things that are happening to the horse's body. It is tied into the loss of impulsion and collection, which in turn are tied to how you use your hands, legs and weight. Elevation starts from behind—your legs and weight, pushing him forward. To comply, the horse drops his hocks beneath his body and drives, propelling himself forward. If at this point you dropped the reins and kept pushing, he would go faster and faster, elongate his neck and body and eventually be running.

But as he drives forward, he meets your hands, which tell him to go no faster (see page 90). Since he has been taught to give to the bridle, as the forward motion carries him into it he gives. However, the forward motion is strong enough that in order to keep from breaching the barrier set by your hands he has to lift his neck and elevate. At the same time, his hocks continue to drive forward, compacting the space his hindquarters take up. That is collection.

You may have seen an example of this a different way if you have ever tried to load a reluctant horse into a horse trailer. The front barrier, to the horse's mind at least, is the wicked horse trailer. Behind him are people driving him forward to it, either with whips or by physically pushing him. He shifts his weight back, scrunches down his rump, and brings his hind legs way beneath his body. His front quarters elevate. Pulling his front quarters up tall is one of his few options, since most of his weight is on his hindquarters, and the barrier keeps him from going any farther forward. He starts looking like a fourteen-hand horse from the rear and a sixteen-hand horse from the front.

Elevation is one of those things that takes experience for the rider

At the stop, walk, trot or canter, the horse should be light on the reins. The reins are the front barrier that aid in elevation and collection. Photograph by Chick Stoll.

to achieve, because it is as much a matter of timing and feel as understanding the application of the cues. What you do must be tailored to what the horse needs for you to do on that particular day, in that particular instant.

The horse starts out his career under saddle unelevated. He cannot learn to elevate until he learns to come off the bit. It is easiest for him to learn to give with his neck in the position that is the most comfortable for him, which may be low. There is nothing wrong with that. When he responds well to the bridle and is collecting, he can begin elevating. Without the first two principles, you cannot teach the third. Teaching him to elevate is a gradual process that relies on his physical structure.

There are two ways to help him elevate. The primary method is squeezing forward to your hands until he not only gives to the bit, but also raises up. This goes back to the earlier discussion about the barrier. If you use too much leg for the amount of hold you have on the reins, the horse will plow through the barrier, your hands, without elevating. If you take too strong a hold for the amount of leg you are using, you will hamper his forward motion, and he will not elevate. The hold presents the barrier, but leaves an opening for him to move forward.

How much to hold and squeeze is a feel you develop with time and practice. It is helpful to recruit someone knowledgeable about English to stand in the middle of the arena when you practice. Have him or her tell you when the horse is losing elevation or fading back off the bit. Pay close attention to what it feels like, then try to collect the horse with your hands and legs and feel for the changes in the horse's body at all gaits. A collected, elevated horse feels tall, buoyant and compact. When he begins the trot, you can feel him pull his body upward and drive forward. The unelevated, uncollected horse feels long and flat. His gaits lack springiness. If he is extremely unelevated, he may even feel as if he is moving downhill.

In the double bridle, when the horse's head drops, use primarily the snaffle to urge it back up. The snaffle is an aid to elevation. When the horse's nose pops out, use a little snaffle or curb and push him to it with your legs. When he's going as he should be, use a balance between the two bits. You will need a shorter hold on the reins at the trot and canter than at the walk. The trot and canter provide more impulsion and elevation. If you were to simply leave your hands in the same position as they were when the horse was walking, as he began to trot he would elevate, creating slack in the rein. Then he would have the opportunity to poke out his nose and string out. When the horse begins a faster gait, you should either shorten your reins or set your hands farther back.

The height you set your hands depends on the horse. Since this is not equitation, you do not have to have a 45-degree bend at the elbows. You can set your hands at the level the horse needs them to be. If he is a compact horse or tends to stick out his nose, you will set your hands lower than if you were riding a horse that has a long, tall neck. Holding your hands higher can help the horse elevate, but keep the horse's build in mind. A short-necked horse is better served by lower hands.

A second way to elevate the horse is to bump one side of the snaffle, or pull upward on it for a moment. This method does not replace the first. It is used on a horse that starts to dip down, or on one that needs a little extra to get him up where he should be. Bumping cannot be your first line of defense because if you bump too much you make the horse's head unsteady. Any bumping should be done as quietly as possible. It is a small movement, not a tremendous yank on the rein.

# 8

# Show Time

HORSES USUALLY MAKE THEIR SHOW debuts after six months or more of good solid work, although the occasional star pupil may do just fine at a show with less time under his cinch than that.

Arrive at the show early to give him a chance to get used to the clamor and distractions, and during the show stick as much as possible to his regular feeding schedule. Horses respond well to routine. You also may want to cover his stall at least in the evening to make sure he takes time out from gawking to sleep. If you've had him in a busy barn at home, the show will not be a major adjustment for him. If the horse has led a sheltered life and is rattled by the environment of the show, cover the stall to give him some down time away from the hubbub, and take him out once or twice daily to see show life in short doses.

Covering the stall is helpful to a horse in a heavily trafficked area. While it is nice for the horse to be able to look out, it also presents some problems. When a lot of people pass by, some will stop and cluck to get his attention or to feed him whatever they are eating. After a few days of this, a horse may become cranky or angry, and his performance may suffer. At most shows, you will not have a problem. If you do, cover the stall. Stall curtains also help people who are looking for your stalls to find them.

Once your horse has settled in, you may want to take advantage of a lunch or dinner break to take him into the main ring before your class. Take a few turns around the arena, and if he does not seem overly spooky at anything, leave the ring and work him in the warmup arena or in the open spaces at the fairgrounds. The less he is in the main ring, the brighter he will look during the class. Everything will be interesting to him, and he will wear his ears forward. By working in the warmup arena you also avoid his associating the main ring with a bad experience or with an extremely hard workout.

It can be difficult to work a horse at a show. In one arena you may see people going in different directions, stock horses sliding past, horses being lunged, and lessons given. In such an environment, you may have more problems with the horse than you did at home. If you have a problem, it's best not to get into an altercation with the horse in the same ring in which you want him to look bright and happy.

The workout should be brief, particularly if you are on a young horse. He does not have the muscle development of a mature horse and will tire more quickly physically and mentally. If he's not ready to show by now, he should have stayed home. Working him an extra hour at the show is not going to make him ready if he was not ready when he came. It makes little sense to work a horse hard for a half hour a day at home, then go to a show and work him for several hours. Save his best for the class. Classes do not last very long, fifteen minutes or so, but during each of those minutes you are asking him for his best, and that takes a lot of effort.

Foster confidence in your horse, and enter the ring at a good collected trot like you mean business. Puttering in like you're not all too sure you should be there is not the way to start a class. Start trotting before you hit the in-gate, and make sure the horse is gathered up and looking like you want him to before he goes in.

When you enter the in-gate, ignore the rail. Go in straight (see page 94). Many people spoil what could have been a really nice entrance because they enter the gate, then swerve over to glue their horses to the rail as soon as possible. It must be instinctual, but whatever it is, it is unnecessary. Corners are the most difficult part of rail work for a horse. He could lose collection, elevation, impulsion, shorten his stride, or do any number of things that make him look bad. There is no point in forcing your horse to do a corner immediately upon entering the ring when it would be easier, and look better, to enter in a straight line.

Your entrance gives the judge his first impression of the horse, and that impression is vital. In a big class, that may be when he decides if he is going to even devote time to watching you. Your job is to catch his attention right then, and make the ride throughout the class worth watching. Some people maneuver to go in the ring first or last. In what order you want to go in is a personal preference. The order is less important than how you go in.

Try to avoid following in a horse you think is more talented than your own. Stay away from that horse throughout the class. Judging is a matter of comparing one horse to another. By riding next to a better horse, you make your horse's shortcomings more obvious.

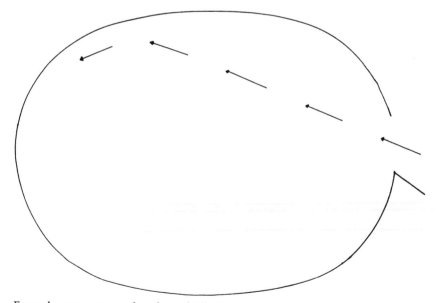

Enter the arena gate and angle gradually over toward the rail, rather than swerving immediately over to the rail.

When the judge looks across the arena, that horse will draw his or her attention. If he or she looks the other way and sees your horse amid a backdrop of the more ordinary horses in the class, yours will look better. The judge still can compare the two of you, but there is no reason to call attention to the fact that you are not quite as good. And it may be that your horse is better than you thought.

Trainers sometimes will cover up each other in the ring. One will ride on the inside track of another, to keep the judge from seeing the other's horse. It is a game best left to those who know how to play it, and are aware who they are playing it with.

Give the judge variety in your rail work. Don't stay on the same place on the rail all the time. Spend some time on the rail, then perhaps move off it for a few revolutions. Go deep in some corners, cut across a few others. Vary the way you reverse from class to class. You can turn into the rail, away from the rail or cut across.

If you are apprehensive about the ride, you've got to put that behind you when you enter the ring. Worrying about how it is all going to come out is a good way to forget all of the things you should be doing to help the horse through the class. You also don't want to give the judge the impression that it is difficult for you to make it through the class, or that these are among the worst minutes of your life. You do not need to keep a fake smile on your face, but do make an effort not to look scared or mad, even if you are.

The judge cannot see everything you feel the horse doing. If you look like you would like to flog your horse in the middle of a class, you may cause the judge to reassess how much of a pleasure your horse is. You also do not want to draw attention to any problems you are having. They are likely to seem more severe to you than to the judge. When judging a quality horse, it is common for judges to overlook problems if the rest of the work is exemplary. The judge may not even have seen whatever horrible error you think occurred. Mistakes can really throw your concentration, but do your best to make the rest of the ride as good as you possibly can. Thinking about a mistake usually just leads to another. If you want to stew about it, do it after the class.

Sometimes you'll see someone in a class have such a bad ride he or she will line up early, or ask to be excused. There are times when you do have to give up, especially if the horse is hurt, or you feel you are endangering yourself, the rest of the class or the horse. If you have had a terrible ride but feel the horse would benefit from completing the class, stick it out unless your presence sabotages other riders' chances at success.

In the ring, the young horse usually feels more secure on the rail, but let the horse's personality and circumstances determine where you place him. If the class is extremely crowded, and the horse is disturbed by other horses brushing past him, you might want to place him more to the inside. If you are riding a small horse in a class of giants, you also may want to keep in mind that he will look larger to the judge's eye if you place him slightly to the inside of the wall.

The rule about where best to place the horse in the ring is about as basic as it gets: Put him where the judge will see him. In crowded classes where the class bears more similarity to bumper cars than any equine pursuit, riders can become so desperate to be seen that they keep moving further and further toward the center of the arena until there is nothing but a swarm of horses making a tiny circle around a judge who occasionally has to step back to keep from being mowed down. The judge should never have to move away from you. If he or she does, you are too close to have made a good impression. You want judges to see your horse, not their lives flashing before their eyes.

Your goal is to present the judge a view of your horse's best as often as possible, with as few horses near you as possible. If you watch an experienced rider in the ring, he or she spends most of the class seemingly without being near anyone else, even in large classes. Nearly anytime the judge looks, there will be a good, clear view of the rider and the horse. That's not luck. It's strategy. The rider puts the horse exactly where he will best be seen by the judge. For a horse to do well in a class, the judge first has to see it.

Stay out of the packs. Horses tend to end up in clusters in a class. If you find yourself in one, circle the horse around to an open spot in the arena, cut across the ring or go deep into a corner so the pack passes you by. When a gait is called, you do not have to perform it that instant. Use gait changes to your advantage. If you've gotten caught in a pack in the canter and the announcer calls for a walk, remain in the canter slightly longer to clear the pack. If you become trapped against the wall in a pack with horses alongside, in front and in back of you, slow the horse down. The judge cannot see you well enough to discern a mild slowing in the gait. The slowing will force the person behind you to go around and allow you to escape. When the way is clear, circle around to get completely clear. Be aggressive. You're out there to show your horse at his best. If there is a pack of horses between you and where you need to be, and you see an opening, plow on through if your horse has the confidence to do it.

This doesn't mean you should be obnoxious in the ring. You can get where you need to be without running over your competitors. Give them the courtesies you wish to be given. It is unprofessional to disrupt another person's horse. Cultivate an awareness of the horses around you in the ring, and avoid passing so close that you brush another horse's body or another rider's body. When going around a horse, avoid cutting so close in front that you disturb the other horse.

A bold, experienced show horse is a joy in a crowded class. He knows how the game works, and you can place him anywhere you want without disrupting him in the slightest. When someone cuts him off in the ring, he just swerves around the obstacle. With the inexperienced horse, you will have to work harder, and avoid potential problem situations. Getting trapped in the middle of a pack with so many horses so close bothers a lot of young horses. Avoid the packs as best you can. If you do find yourself in a tough situation, use more hand and leg to keep him together through it. If a horse in your class is having obvious problems, cut across the ring and get away from him. You don't want to get caught up in his mess.

When it is time to line up, trot right on up to the line, then make the transition quickly down to the stop. It looks much better than trotting in a ways, dribbling down to a walk, then kind of wandering over like you've gotten lost. Movements should be decisive. Park the horse straight, and in alignment with the other horses. Insist that the horse stand there quietly. Do not let him rest a foot. If he starts wiggling around, check him back with your hands. If that does not work, bump him with your legs, too, or tap him with the whip. Absence of pressure is a reward. Don't reward him for his impatience by throwing him rein and hoping he stands still.

When the judge speaks to you in the lineup, make eye contact. Give him or her a little smile if you like. It also is considered polite for men to remove their hats when being addressed by a female judge. If asked to back the horse, back straight.

Judging continues in the lineup until the judge's card is turned in to the announcer. See that your horse looks his best at all times when in the arena. If you receive a ribbon, gather up the horse and trot forward energetically to get it. Smile. Pet the horse. He worked pretty hard, after all. Wandering over to pick up the ribbon makes you seem indifferent, and arrogant. If you are enjoying yourself, share the good time with the people watching. There aren't any rules that say riders have to be stoic or aloof.

If you didn't do well, trot out of the ring with an energy and flare that will make the judge wonder why he or she didn't place you higher. You may be showing under that judge again sometime.

Try to limit the classes you go in to two or three per horse. English requires tremendous effort from the horse. For the horse to be brilliant and really give you all he has, you have to limit his classes. He can go in a lot more than two or three, but the more you take him in, the less he will be able to give you.

At small shows, the lesser effort will be enough, but as you go higher in competition, you will need every ounce of energy and brilliance he has. This is a very competitive field. At one time English horses also went in Western and a whole range of other classes, and had plenty of go left over for their English classes. Times have changed. Selective breeding for English characteristics have brought such advancement in the abilities of the horses that the jack-of-all-trades is rare. The English horses have become specialists, because in order to be competitive they have to put out the ultimate effort in every class. Training has to be very focused.

People with young horses often bombard them with classes because they need the experience. They do need experience, but they also tire quickly. Limit their classes. Taking a young horse in class after class to the point of exhaustion is one of the surest ways to sour him to the ring.

The veteran should also go only in a few classes a show. He already has experience and does not need another turn around the ring to make him better. In general, the less he is in the main ring, the better he will be when it really counts. Unless for your own peace of mind you need to ride in the main ring as a warmup for the class, keep the veteran out of the main ring altogether until his class goes in. If the horse goes in never having seen the interior of the ring before, there is a greater chance his ears will be up, and he will look brighter.

# 9

# Problems, Problems

EVERYBODY HAS PROBLEMS AT SOME point. Sometimes the horse is just having a bad day, and sometimes it is a lasting problem. You have to decide whether it's worth fighting over, or if can you get around the fight and still make your point. If you can avoid serious fights without losing ground to the horse, so much the better. Horses seem to remember every bad thing that ever happens to them. Try to keep the workouts from becoming one of those traumatic memories.

If your horse is usually fairly responsive, but for some reason is being obnoxious and pushy on a certain day, he may not feel well, or may just be having an off day. Try to find something he can do well and end the workout after he performs the task adequately. You might just want to get off and bit him up or long-line him.

If it is a problem that has cropped up time and time again, work him until he gets it right or comes close to it. Then get off and reward him by ending the workout. It does not necessarily have to be perfect.

The important thing is that he shows improvement.

Some problems have little to do with the horse being obstinate or not understanding what you are trying to get him to do. In the show ring you sometimes see horses that bob their heads or have gait irregularities. The head should always be steady, and the gait without any hops, skips or uneven strides.

Bobbing of the head can be caused by lameness. It depends on the rhythm of the bob. If the head is going up with one leg and down with another, the horse is lame. Consult a veterinarian. If his head is bobbing in time with both legs, going up and down with each stride, he probably is not lame. You may want to have a vet check him anyway, however. More than likely the horse is using his head to pump himself along, the way birds do when they walk. If he is doing this, he is not moving forward and giving to the bridle properly. He needs to be driven forward more strongly and balanced with the hands. You may find it helpful to bit him up and drive him to the bit from behind, to review for him the principles of moving forward and giving to the bridle. A bobbing head may also be caused by a rider with unsteady hands that are bumping the reins in time with the strides.

When the horse has irregular gaits, the first thing to consider is lameness. Irregularities to watch for include a horse's taking a longer stride with one leg than the other, making a skipping motion with the hind legs, or in the middle of the trot breaking down into a scrambling trot of frantic, short strides and then resuming the regular trot.

Lunge the horse, and if an irregularity is apparent, consult a veterinarian. Even if one is not, there may be a physical problem that shows up only under saddle. You may want to have the vet watch you ride the horse.

If the vet does not find anything, then it is likely you are unintentionally causing the problem by the way you ride. You may want to seek assistance to pinpoint the problem. The horse that is taking a longer stride on one side than the other (the long one usually is to the inside) is unbalanced. Look for the most obvious causes first. Are you sitting straight on the horse, or are you tipping your body to the side or twisting your torso? Are you posting straight up, or crooked? Are you holding one rein hand much higher than the other? (There are occasions when you will have one higher than the other for a short period of time, but if you have them that way all the time, you could be causing the horse problems.)

Uneven strides can also be caused by squeezing the horse forward without giving proper support with the reins. The horse rushes forward without a good feel of where the barrier is, or finds the barrier in the wrong place for good balance. Unbalanced, the horse flops along, taking one big stride, then catching up to that stride with a quick little one.

Inadequate hand/leg coordination also can cause the other two problems. The horse that skips along with his hind legs trying to catch up to the front is being rushed forward without being balanced. The horse that scrabbles is not getting the support he needs from the rider. He goes along fine for a while, then loses his impulsion and collection and has to scramble to get back into stride.

The problem is most likely to show up in a corner, when balance is easiest to lose. Don't oversqueeze in the corners. As you go in, rate the horse back slightly and use your inside leg and hand to bend him to the curve of the corner. If he is moving forward well and is collected, you will need much less leg than if he is bogging down.

Your response to him has to fit the circumstances. Pummeling him with your leg when all he needs is a little squeeze is going to cause gait problems. So will not using enough leg when he needs a lot. Symptoms that you are not getting the job done in the corner are gait irregularities, a bobbing head, and feeling his body elongate. You may even hear the sharp click of a hind hoof hitting a front. Any of these could mean he is not collected, not balanced. Reassess how you are executing your corners. Practice them at the walk, then at a moderate trot or at a sitting trot to get the hang of how he should balance and feel.

# KEEPING SPICE IN THE RELATIONSHIP

To the young horse, each day is new and different, and he is bright with the excitement and wonder of it all. The simplest things impress him: he'll perk his ears at practically anything, and when the show ring announcer calls for the walk, he walks along without anticipating the next gait.

But soon the bloom begins to fade. After a few shows, he figures out that the walk is followed by a trot or canter, and he becomes less patient to wait for you to give the cue. If you are not on guard, the walking horse will launch himself into the next gait at any crackle of the loudspeaker. Since he listens more for the sound than the words spoken, you could prematurely find yourself trotting when the loud-speaker announces the annual show watermelon feed.

After a season, he thinks he knows far more than you do. After a few more seasons, nothing looks as interesting as it once did. After still more, his ears stay back against his head, except when the class is over and he is trotting out the gate. The brightness that made him sparkle in the ring is gone. Replacing it is a look of cranky boredom at having to take yet another person around a circle he's traveled a thousand times.

That is how it can be with the veteran, but not how it should be. He can retain that brightness and willingness with a little help from you. He's bored. Why should he put his ears up in the ring when he's been around the corner a thousand times? He knows what's around it. Why look? He's done the same thing day after day for years and he's tired of it all. He needs to be challenged, to see different things and to do different things.

At the show, the veteran does not need to spend hours going around the practice arena. He knows the way around already. He does need to be worked at the show to keep him tuned, but the workout should be fairly short, twenty minutes or so, unless a problem surfaces. If he is not working properly, then of course keep going until he is.

At home keep the veteran out of the ring as much as possible. Work him outside in fields or along lanes, or go for a ride in the woods (see page 103). You can work him and have a pleasurable ride out at the same time. He'll enjoy it more, and so will you. His ears will be up because there is something new and interesting to look at every day. Work in through all of the gaits, do some exercises, and play with him. See how many "gears" he has. Boost him into a canter, then see just how far you can slow it down. Then do a hand gallop. Bring him down to a walk. Urge him into his fastest walk, then slow it to a moderate walk. Do a normal trot, then an extended trot, then a sitting trot, asking for the same collection but less speed. There are all kinds of things you can do to make workouts varied and interesting.

The horse should also get a chance to play without you. If he is confined in a stall, turn him out regularly for some free time. It is also good for him to be long-lined for many of the workouts instead of ridden. You'll get to see how he looks from the ground, and he can work without contending with your weight. You may even want eventually to hook him to a buggy and try a new class.

Practice the horse outside the arena whenever possible to prevent burnout. Practicing in more interesting surroundings is one of the elements that has helped keep show veteran Canadian Love bright and highly competitive in the ring. Photograph by Chick Stoll.

# 10

# Looking Sharp

"DRESS FOR SUCCESS" APPLIES JUST as much to the show ring as it does to the business world. After spending hours grooming the horse and months of training, getting him ready for that instant when the two of you will enter the ring, it makes little sense not to put just as much thought into your own appearance. With clothing you can enhance your strong points, those of the horse, and enhance the image of the two of you as a team.

Chose outfits that are tasteful, neat and becoming to you and the horse. Turn through this book and look at the various people in show attire. They all look professional, tidy and elegant. That is the same effect you want to achieve.

Before you begin shopping for an outfit, have in mind the overall look you wish to create, and the colors you want. If you don't have a plan, you may spend more money than you intended and have an outfit that does not look well. You may find it helpful to attend a few shows and look at the clothes being worn. Try to determine why you like a particular outfit. Look beyond just the color of the riding coat.

It's likely that part of the reason you find the coat pleasing is because it coordinates with the horse, rider and other parts of the outfit. How would an outfit like that look on your horse? How would it look on you? Are you at a level of riding that you can wear something like that? Do you attend shows where such an outfit is appropriate?

Although looking at other riders is a good way to get ideas for apparel, you will want clothes that meet your own needs and those of the horse. Talk to representatives at apparel companies, and look at fabric samples. Most shops do not charge consultation fees. The clothing professional can alert you to the best fabrics, trends in riding clothes and what is available. It's useful to have a picture of your horse with you when you want to select clothes.

If you are new to the show ring and have no idea what you need or why you need it, find a mentor. Along with talking to clothing professionals, also talk to a trainer or to an experienced amateur rider in your area. No doubt they will be glad to help you pick out what you need. Somewhere down the line, someone helped them get started and many are happy to return the favor. If you are going to make your own riding attire, it still is helpful to go through all of these steps.

The English rider wears a derby or soft hat, a shirt, tie, collar clasp, saddle coat, vest, gloves, riding jodhpurs and jodhpur boots (see page 106). For the outfit to look sharp, all of these elements must fit properly and be color-coordinated (see page 107). Always make sure the clothes you wear into the ring are clean, tidy and appropriate for the class you are attending.

# HAT

Three styles of hats currently are worn in the ring: the derby (see page 107), homburg (see page 108) and snap-brim (see page 108). The snap-brim resembles a hat that Humphrey Bogart might have worn—with the brim turned up in the back and down in the front. The homburg has a narrower and more shaped brim that is turned up all the way around.

Proper attire for English Pleasure. The coat should be color coordinated to look good with both horse and rider and match the hat, here a homburg. A tie in harmony with the colors of the vest and coat, dark gloves, conservative jodhpurs and a small flower complete the ensemble. Photograph by Jim Bortvedt.

A number of things detract from this attire: no gloves, a wrist strap on the whip, a shirt collar that is too big, an inappropriate hair ornament, a coat that is a bit too short and jodhpurs that are too short. Photographer unknown.

A derby.

A homburg.

A snapbrim.

Women wear derbies (in equitation, the derby is mandatory) and homburgs. Men prefer the snap-brim, and for a more formal look wear a homburg.

An improperly sized hat can ruin an otherwise good outfit. The hat should fit the head snugly but not be too tight or too loose. A hat that is losing its shape also detracts from the overall effect. Have your hat blocked at the beginning of every show season, and several times throughout. It makes a considerable difference to the appearance.

Most riders wear hats that match either their jodhpurs or their coats.

There are a number of companies that will custom-dye hats any color, but keep to the same color family as the rest of your outfit. For example, don't wear a navy blue suit with coordinating shirt and tie, and then top it off with a bright red hat because you wanted to add more color. The hat is not the place to add more color.

Select a dark color for your hat if you are fairly tall for the size of your horse. Light hats draw attention to your height. White hats and other light-colored hats should only be worn by very experienced riders. The light shades draw attention to every movement of the head. If you have any doubt about what color hat to wear, match it to your jodhpurs.

# SHIRT

The shirt is the same type that a businessman might wear to an important meeting. It should have that crisp look of a newly starched shirt and be in a color that coordinates well with the suit. White and pastels are popular.

It should also fit nicely around the neck. Men's shops generally carry shirts with collars 14½ inches and above. If you need anything smaller, you will have to shop in the boy's department, at a riding apparel shop, or have the shirt tailor made. You may be able to find a suitable shirt in the women's department or in a mail-order catalog, but this can present problems since the collars are often too short to look good with a tie. Plain dress collars that do not button down are preferred.

Formal wear, a wing-collar shirt with a bow tie, is acceptable for evening classes at the larger shows.

Don't wear shirts that are lacy or ruffly. With the English-style suit, a plain shirt is much more elegant.

# TIE

Select a tie that a conservatively dressed businessman might wear. The tie should be in harmony with the colors of the suit and shirt. It should not be too narrow or too short. A bow tie can be worn for a more formal look in the evening classes at larger shows.

# COLLAR CLASP

The clasp passes beneath the knot of the tie to connect the shirt collar. It makes for a neat appearance and is one of the many small things that contribute to an overall tasteful look. Collar clasps can be purchased in any men's shop.

# SADDLE COAT

The most important aspect about a coat is that it fit well. If it is too big, too small, too short, too narrow in the shoulders or too tight across the waist, it simply will not look good. The coat is a vital part of your look and will be the most expensive part of your outfit, whether you make it, buy it off the rack or have it tailor made.

People often make the mistake of buying a suit that will not fit them properly when they are on the horse. Sleeves that seemed long enough in the store suddenly are way too short when you get on the horse, because you ride with your arms bent.

When trying on the coat, bend your arms as if you are riding. The sleeve should reach to where your wrists join the arm bones. The shirt cuffs should not show below the sleeve. The coat should also feel comfortable across the shoulders and around the waist.

The button that closes the jacket should be at your waist, an inch or so above your navel. If it buttons much higher than that, or, if you have difficulty buttoning it, the jacket is too small. You are going to be riding a horse in this jacket—it has to be comfortable.

The bottom of the coat should reach down to immediately above the bend in your knee. When you are mounted on the horse, the coat should fall across the center of your knee. A common error is to make the coat or the vent too short. The vent should be deep enough to make the jacket part smoothly around the saddle and horse's rump.

# VEST

The vest gives the outfit a much tidier look. Although a vest is not required under AHSA rules, at the moderate to large shows few riders go without a vest.

The vest can be the same color as the jacket, or be a coordinating color. Many riders favor wearing a solid coat, with a vest that is a plaid or other pattern. You also can wear a patterned coat with a solid vest. Reversible vests—those with a different color on each side—are very popular.

The vest should be well tailored to the body, and be long enough to go over the waistband of the jodhpurs. If you have trouble buttoning it, it is too small.

# GLOVES

Gloves serve two purposes: they make an outfit look more polished and the movements of your hands less obvious. Gloves should always be worn. Dark gloves that are color-coordinated with your jacket are best. The lighter the color, the more the movements of your hands will be noticed. If you have extraordinarily still hands, you can wear any color you like, even white; otherwise, stay away from light colors.

Buy leather gloves that fit smoothly over the hand. Gloves made of stretch fabrics look nice and cost less, but they can make it harder to hold the reins. Leather gloves are worth the price difference. Even with leather gloves, you may have more difficulty with the reins than you did barehanded.

# JODHPURS

Jodhpurs should fit loosely in the seat and legs, then bell out over the boot. Remember that they are meant to fit well while you are sitting on a horse, not standing in a fitting room. There, they should look way too long and loose, but not baggy in the seat. The bell at the bottom should be cut so the fabric will cover the heel of the boot when you are sitting on the horse.

If you are buying jodhpurs off the rack, when trying them on squat down or straddle a chair like you are on a horse. Make sure they feel comfortable and are long enough. When you are riding, the pants are kept from creeping up your leg by an elastic jodhpur strap that attaches to buttons just inside the bottom of the pant leg, then passes under the heel of the boot. Some straps are fastened with a clip inside the pant instead of a button.

## BOOTS

Jodhpur boots are ankle high and come in black and brown leather and patent leather. Patent leather is favored at the larger shows. If your feet tend to wobble, you may not want to call attention to them by wearing patent leather.

## ACCESSORIES

Any accessories, such as a flower in the lapel or hair ribbon, should be small and tasteful.

Most riders carry whips in the ring. The whip should be thin, about three feet long, and have a "mushroom cap" handle. This small metal cap keeps the whip from sliding through your hand and dropping to the ground. The cap serves the same purpose as a wrist strap but looks far better.

Spurs, if you wear any, should be small and of English type.

## SELECTING COLORS AND PATTERNS

Color is a matter of individual taste, but there are some guidelines to help you select what will flatter you and the horse. Keep in mind that your favorite color may not necessarily make up into a pleasing outfit. Evaluate color in terms of your complexion and your horse's color.

Also consider your own level of skill and that of the horse. The horse might look stunning in a showy coat, but he has to be ready for the attention before you wear that coat in the ring. For example, if he is a young horse that has trouble getting the proper lead, you might want to fade into the background or hide behind a group of horses when it is time to pick up the lead. You cannot do that successfully if you are wearing a coat that shouts "Look over here!"

The same rule applies to you. If you lack experience, have a lot of movement in your riding or tend to have a few bobbles in the ring, pick a more conservative color. You do not want to be a bright spot in the ring unless you can take the scrutiny. Stay away from white and bright colors. The judge will still watch you, but will be less likely to notice your mistakes.

If you are heavy, avoid plaids and large patterns. Darker colors will make you look slimmer and more elegant.

Pick one color as the base you will match the other parts of your outfit to. It should be a color that will allow you to expand the number of looks you can present without buying much more clothing. Navy blue, deep burgundy and black are good base colors. There are very few colors that don't go with them.

Currently, brightly colored print or pastel coats are very popular with women, but men are still wearing primarily dark suits. For a man, woman, boy or girl, the dark suit is always correct and proper in any English class. If you are just starting out, the dark suit is probably your best bet. It always looks elegant and does not draw attention to your mistakes. The conservative suit is a requirement for youth riding English equitation.

In the beginning, the dark jacket, vest and jodhpurs will serve you well. As you progress in your riding skills, you can build on the outfit. Keeping the jodhpurs as a base color, you can add a coat of a complementary color. With just that one change, the whole outfit takes on a different look. Still another look can be achieved by adding a plaid vest that picks up the color of both jodhpurs and jacket. Building on the base color, you can get a number of outfits while spending a minimum amount of money. Avoid combining more than two or three colors in one outfit.

Select colors appropriate for your age. If you are riding in the youth divisions, avoid loud colors. Dress either in a conservative suit or pastels. Parents should not buy "cute" riding clothes for their children. Instead, they should wear conservative colors or pastels and the same kind of shirt, tie and suit an adult would wear. They'll still be cute. Since children grow so fast, parents might want to advertise in riding magazines or newspapers for particular sizes, or offer to sell or trade the last set of clothes their children outgrew. Many cost-conscious parents are looking to buy and offering to sell children's used riding clothes.

Buy with an eye for quality. Riding clothes take a lot of abuse and must be tough. Among the best fabrics for riding clothes are wools, wool blends and silks. The silks take more care than wool but make beautiful coats that are very popular in the show ring.

When planning your attire, remember that the person you are trying to impress is the judge. You must look good at a distance. Don't pick out a particular pattern just because it has interesting little squiggles in it. The judge is never going to see the squiggles. How does it look from a distance of thirty feet or so? If it is rather bland from that distance, select something else. Pick colors that will go with any horse's color. Through your show career you may have many different horses.

As your skills improve and you are mounted on increasingly better horses, the attire can get bolder, brighter. For an experienced rider on a high-powered horse, there is almost no limit to the patterns and colors that will look sharp and stress the pair's best qualities.

# 11

# Show Structure and Regulations

M Y FIRST BRUSH WITH THE class list and entry form for a Class A Arabian show was exciting and demoralizing at the same time. More than a hundred classes were listed (at least half of which I thought my poor, grossly overworked 4-H horse was qualified to enter), and the entry blank was nearly incomprehensible. After a few shows, however, I realized that the entry blanks for rated shows and the workings of the shows themselves are very similar. After dealing with the first entry and show, you will find that the rest are easy—from the tiny local show up to the Nationals.

## STRUCTURE

The American Horse Shows Association authors the rules used in all shows approved by the association, including the majority of Arabian shows in the United States. The International Arabian Horse

Association (IAHA) conducts the shows through member clubs and plays a role in the making of the AHSA rules relating to Arabian horses. In Canada the show rules used are those of the Canadian Equestrian Federation.

Both the AHSA and IAHA publish magazines that are sent to members to keep them current. Both organizations publish annual rule books. Although sweeping changes in the rules are rare, rules do get modified or altered and new rules get added. Rule books also contain information that is important, such as how to properly measure the length of a hoof.

Arabian shows in the United States are rated A or B based on a number of factors, including prize money offered and the number of certain kinds of classes in specific divisions. The highest rating is A, followed by B, with an unrated show the lowest. One show can have several different ratings, for example, Class A for Arabians, but Class B for Half-Arabians because it lacks sufficient Half-Arabian classes.

All of the approved shows must have judges that have been approved. IAHA provides a list of these judges in the IAHA Handbook. The show must also have an official steward to assist the judge, and it must be run according to the AHSA rules.

## FINDING THE SHOWS

When you first begin showing, it will take work to get the premium books (class lists and entry forms) for shows. The following year after your first show, the premium book will be sent to you automatically. It is just a matter of getting on the show's mailing list.

To get a premium book for a show you have never attended, watch the horse magazines for listings of shows. The various Arabian magazines and those published by the IAHA and AHSA all contain calendars of shows. Listed with the show and date is the name of the horse show secretary. You can write to or call that person to receive a premium book. There is no charge for the book.

It will contain all of the information you need to know to enter the show and find the show grounds. If you are new to showing, make sure to read the class descriptions before entering. The descriptions will tell you what will be expected of you. Also before going to a show, whether you are a beginner or veteran, take note of who the judge is. You may want to keep a running list of the judges who liked your horse and those who did not. Showing takes a fair amount of effort and money, regardless of how you do. You might as well show under judges who favor your horse.

# THE ENTRY BLANK

The blank asks for the horse's name, breed, registration number, age, sex, color and height. It also asks for the name and registration of the sire and that of the dam (see page 118). All the information needed to fill this out can be found in the horse's registration papers. You will have to submit a copy of those papers along with the entry blank.

The form asks for the name, IAHA number and AHSA number of the rider. The two organizations issue cards to their members yearly. The numbers are on the cards. Send a photocopy of the cards in with the entry blank. If you are not a member of either of these organizations, you still can enter the show, but you will be charged an extra fee per horse for each membership you are lacking. This gets costly after a while. If you are going to show much, it is to your advantage to join the two organizations.

For information about joining the IAHA, you can telephone 303-450-4774, or write to the International Arabian Horse Association, P.O. Box 33696, Denver, CO, 80233-0696. To learn about joining the AHSA, telephone 212-972-2472, or write the American Horse Shows Association, 220 East 42nd Street, New York, NY 10017. They will send you a membership application and information.

Farther down on the entry form, it asks for the name of the owner or agent, his or her IAHA and AHSA numbers, the farm name, address, telephone number and the owner's signature. It may also ask for his or her social security number. Again, make sure you have photocopies of all of these cards. The form asks for the same information about the trainer. If you do not have a trainer, write in the name of the person who works with the horse the most.

Amateur riders must give their amateur numbers, which is on the AHSA card. Parents have to sign their permission for amateurs under eighteen to ride.

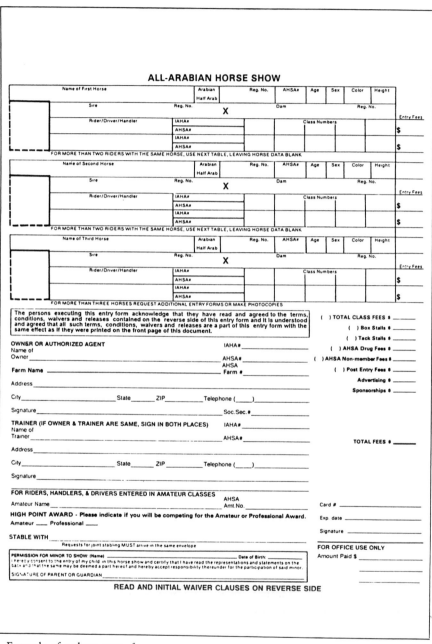

Example of a show entry form.

Next on the blank you will come to the fees, and there are a lot of them. First are the per class fees. They are fairly straightforward and are listed in the premium book along with the class lists. Stall fees are listed next and tend to be costly. You may pay more for a stall than you do for entry fees. If you want a separate stall to store your tack (a common practice at larger shows), you might pay the same fee you paid for the horse's stall—but usually it is a larger fee—even though the tack stall occupies the same amount of space as the horse uses, and you are sparing the show the cost of the bedding. Stall fees earn lots of grumbles from competitors.

Somewhere on the form it may also ask if you want to be stabled near someone else. At some shows there is a charge for the privilege. The show secretary's name and number will be listed on the entry blank, and you can ask him or her if a fee will be charged.

Additional fees abound on the entry blank. The AHSA drug fee is a set fee that funds drug-testing efforts at the show. You pay the fee whether your horse is among those tested or not. Horses are routinely tested at the shows for any forbidden drugs.

Also among the lists of fees are post entries. Post-entry fees are those you pay if you are entering after the entries were due. Avoid late entries if you can. Post entries are often double the usual entry fees.

There may also be fees listed for advertising, sponsorships and cattle. Unless you want to advertise, sponsor a class (fund the expense of ribbons and trophy) or enter a class where cattle are used, ignore these.

On the back of the entry form may be one or more waivers requiring your signature. Basically, they state that the information you have given is correct, that you are bound by AHSA and IAHA rules and that the show is not responsible for any injuries or losses at the show.

## AT THE SHOW

Arrive at the show with plenty of time to spare before your first class. Whenever you have to travel a long distance, it is a good idea to go a day or more before the show to give you and your horse a chance to settle in. When you get to the grounds, find the horse show office. The office workers will give you a packet with your number, a list of classes entered and anything else you need at the show. You will be given a number for each horse shown. The number follows the horse into all his classes, regardless of who rides him. The exception is in equitation classes, where the number follows the rider into all the equitation classes, regardless of the horse ridden.

At large shows, the packet may also include parking permits and passes to allow you to watch classes without being charged spectator admission fees. The office workers can also tell you where you are stabled or refer you to the office that handles stabling. Should you arrive at the show after the office has closed, you will find that stabling assignments are posted on a bulletin board near the office or tags are on the stall doors.

Most shows span two or three days, although the large ones can last more than a week. Morning classes usually begin around 8:00 A.M. and will go until they conclude. It is hoped that they will be over before the 1:00 P.M. classes are due to begin, but that does not always happen. When morning classes run overtime, the afternoon classes usually start an hour after the morning ones are concluded. If the morning classes conclude early, afternoon classes will begin at their scheduled time.

Most shows also have night classes that begin around 6:00 or 7:00 P.M. At a large show, these classes can run quite late. It is fairly common for the last class to be concluded at 11:00 P.M. or even midnight. AHSA rules forbid any classes to begin after midnight and require at least eight hours between the last class of the evening and the first class the next morning.

Breaks in between classes are good times to try out the arena, get a quick bite to eat while you have the chance or take in the various festivities. Many shows have a variety of social functions between classes or late at night. They include ice cream socials, barbecues, dances, parties and open houses at the stables of farms at the show. They are part of what makes showing fun and will give you a chance to meet the other exhibitors and talk horses.

The classes you will show in are of two types: regular classes and championships. Certain classes qualify you to go into the championships. For example, early in the premium book will be listed English Pleasure Open, and later the English Pleasure Open Championship. Competing in the first, no matter how you place, qualifies you for the second. Other classes may as well. The premium book will list which classes qualify. You do not do anything different in the championship than you do in the regular classes, but the ribbons and awards are nicer, and the class may have a purse.

At small, unrated shows, it is not uncommon for the order of classes or for the times they begin to be shifted around. This is against the rules at rated shows. All classes must be held in the order listed unless at least twelve hours notice is given to competitors.

# GATE HOLDS AND TIME-OUTS

Under normal circumstances, you will try to arrive at the gate prior to your class and allow enough time to warm up your horse, check in with the gate attendant and get into your class in a timely manner. But events at shows aren't always normal. Occasionally, you will find yourself unable to make it to your class on time. This could happen if your classes fall one right after another, and you do not have sufficient time to make a tack or clothing change. You can gain a few extra minutes by asking the person tending gate for a gate hold. A gate hold gives you three additional minutes to make it to your class. That does not sound like much, but it can make the difference between making your class and missing it. You must arrange for this prior to the class, however.

Once in the class, if you have a problem with your equipment, such as a loose saddle or broken tack, you can call for a time-out. Ride to the middle of the ring and request it from the ring stewart. You will be given a maximum of five minutes *per class* to take care of the problem, and you can be assisted by two attendants. You can call no more that two time-outs. If one lasts two minutes, your second cannot last any longer than three.

A time-out also can be called if your horse throws a shoe. A farrier will put the shoe back on while the rest of the class waits; then the class will resume. For a cast shoe, your five-minute allotment begins when the farrier enters the ring or touches the shoe, whichever happens first. If the shoe is weighed, the time that procedure takes is not included.

During a time-out, judging is suspended. The other competitors can work their horses at any gaits they please or make adjustments on their own equipment. When someone in your class calls a time-out, use the time to your advantage. If you didn't have enough time to warm the horse up prior to the class, do it during the time-out. If he's tired, drop down to a walk and save his energy for the class. If he's pushing on your hands or feels stiff, do a few exercises, such as circles.

# DRUG USE

In general, the AHSA forbids the use of any stimulant, depressant, tranquilizer, local anesthetic, drug or drug metabolite that might affect the performance of the horse. It also forbids any drug that may interfere with the detection of another drug. Complete drug regulations are listed in the AHSA Rule Book.

Random testing of the horses is fairly routine, especially at the larger shows. The tests are quite sensitive and can pick up even small traces of caffeine—including the amount that would be in the horse's blood if you shared a Pepsi with him. Don't share any food with your horse at a show, especially if it contains caffeine or chocolate. Chocolate, for example, has a number of substances that show up in drug tests. The amount of the substance in the horse's blood from sharing a snack may not be enough to affect performance, but it is better to avoid sharing snacks than to have a positive drug test and go through the resulting hassle.

Some drugs, such as phenylbutazone, are permitted within tight limits for therapeutic purposes. Some forbidden drugs can also be used. It must be documented, however, that such a drug is necessary for the treatment of an illness or injury; that the horse will not compete until at least twenty-four hours after being given the drug; that the drug is given by a vet (or a trainer if the vet isn't available), and you must write down the vital statistics, such as the name of the medication, when it was given, the horse it was given to, etc.

There are so many drugs on the market that the AHSA does not publish a list of all the illegal drugs. Avoid all drugs unless there is a definite medical need. If you must use a drug and do not know if it is restricted, call the AHSA's drug information line: 1-800-MED-AHSA.

When a forbidden substance is found in the horse's blood, the AHSA calls a hearing. If evidence shows that a drug was given to alter the horse's performance, the owner must surrender all prizes, money and points won, and pay a fine. The trainer involved may be fined and suspended from all competition for a period of time.

# REGIONALS

The United States and Canada are divided into eighteen regions for the purpose of having regional championship shows. Most regions comprise several states. Region V, for example, takes in Washington, Alaska and parts of Montana and Idaho. California is so densely populated with horses and people that it contains three of the eighteen regions: Regions I, II and III. A map of the regions is published in the IAHA handbook.

A regional show is more prestigious than a regular show and may employ a number of judges for one class. To qualify for a regional class, the horse must have placed first or second in that specific class at a Class A or B show in that region within the last two years. You can attend as many regional shows as you want, regardless of where you live, but for each of those regions you must qualify the horse in that region. Winning English Pleasure Open in Region I only qualifies you to enter the English Pleasure Open Regional I Championship class. You can't enter the same class in Region II unless you qualify in II.

In open classes, only the horse must qualify. It does not matter if a different person rides him in the regional class. That does not hold true in Amateur Owner to Ride classes. Since only an amateur who owns the horse can ride this class, the same rider qualifies the horse and rides him in the regionals. If the horse is sold after qualifying, his new amateur owner can ride him in the regionals without requalifying.

If you just can't get qualified before the regionals, many regional shows do offer you a last chance to win that qualification. They conduct regular Class A classes at the same show as the regional classes. If you qualify in one of these classes, you will not have to pay a post entry fee for the regional class, even though the entry deadline has passed.

In a regional championship, the rail work is the same as in a regular class, although the competition tends to be of a higher caliber than at a regular show. The award title of Top Five is given to the top five horses in the class, and then Champion and Reserve Champion are awarded.

# NATIONALS

Each year the United States Arabian and Half-Arabian Championship alternates sites between sprawling grounds in Louisville, Kentucky, and Albuquerque, New Mexico. The Canadian Arabian and Half-Arabian Championship, always held in August, has been at a number of sites, including Edmonton, Alberta, a few miles away from the world's largest shopping mall, and Regina, Saskatchewan, where the ring rests on top of an ice skating rink. The Canadian Nationals tend to be smaller than the United States Nationals.

When you qualify to go to the Nationals, you are qualified to go to either one, or both. The Nationals give the horse enthusiast the opportunity to see the best horses of Canada and the United States and to compete against them. Even if you are not showing, it is a delight just to attend and watch the classes.

There are two ways to qualify. The least complicated method is to win a Top Five at a regional show. By attending a few regional shows you'll know if you are ready to go to the Nationals. Frankly, if you cannot win the Top Five it takes to qualify, your chances at the Nationals are slim.

You also can qualify by accumulating points by placing in regular show classes, but since the number of points you get depends in part on the number of horses in the class, the shows you attend must be fairly large for this system to be efficient. If you are going to small shows, it will take quite some time and a lot of wear on your horse to get all the points you need. A list of points and the system used to acquire them are in the IAHA Handbook.

At the nationals, competitors first ride in a number of preliminary classes. With each class, more and more horses are eliminated until there are around twenty horses competing for Top Ten. Once the Top Ten horses in the nation in that class are selected, the Top Ten will ride for the title of National Champion, and National Reserve Champion. A national championship is the highest pinnacle that can be reached with an English horse at a single show.

# SCOTTSDALE

The Scottsdale All Arabian Show, held in mid February every year, is the most prestigious non-national show in the United States. It lasts more than a week and is preceded by horse auctions that range from casual to black tie. The Scottsdale show has the reputation of being among the best places to market a horse, horse shop, and get a glimpse of the rising stars of the coming season. No qualification is required to enter the show.

The highest pinnacle a show horse can reach in one season is to win the championship at Scottsdale in February, the championship at the Canadian Nationals in August, and the championship at the U.S. Nationals in October. It's sometimes called the Triple Crown, and such three-way wins are few and far between.

# KEEPING SHOW RECORDS

You may think that you will remember forever the glorious moment you receive a ribbon. It may be true of some shows, but not all of them. Writing down the show and placings is essential if you want a permanent record.

Include in your record the horse's name, rider's name, judge, official name of show, date, a list of classes participated in (including those you bombed out in), placings in those classes, any prize money won and special awards such as high-point gelding of the show. If you are counting points to go to the Nationals, or to receive a year-end high-point award of some type, also include the number of horses in the class.

# 12

# Show Grooming

WHEN YOU ENTER A SHOW ring, you are just one of many vying for the judge's attention. To be a contender, you have to do everything you can to look like one.

Grooming weaves illusion into reality. Beauticians and makeup artists work according to the same principle. Sometime at a show go to the stall of a horse you found particularly beautiful in the ring and see what he looks like without of his "makeup," with a manure stain on the side of his head and his mane and tail tangled with wood shavings. It would be even more fun to see him in the dead of winter after he's spent several months in a muddy pasture and looks a lot more like a musk ox than a horse. A beautiful horse is always beautiful, but grooming can make a considerable difference in appearance.

Before you start clipping and grooming, stand back and take a look at your horse. What are his best features to emphasize? What are his worst features to hide?

# CLIPPING

Generally, if the horse has a good, short, summer coat only the head and legs are clipped. If the horse looks a bit shaggy, the entire body may be clipped. The clippers should be of a type designed for animals and have interchangeable blades. The blades commonly available are 10, 15, 30, and 40. Of these, 40 is the finest, 10 the coarsest.

On the legs, use a 30 or 40 blade around the coronet band of the hoof, then switch to the 10 blade for the leg up to the knee (see page 128). Blend the clipped hair into the hair directly beneath the knee to hide the transition in the contour of the leg. When doing the hind legs, clip up to the hocks. When clipping, overlap the strokes of the blade as evenly as possible to keep the clipper marks to a minimum. Many horses, especially bays and chestnuts, are a different color beneath the hair from on the surface. Uneven strokes and gouges in the hair show. You may want to clip the legs a to week or two before the show to give the hair a chance to grow out a bit. This will ease the clipper marks and restore some of the color and shine to the legs. Unless given a chance to grow out, white stockings will look pink because of the color of the skin beneath.

After finishing all four legs, use the 10 blade to tidy up any shaggy areas on the horse. Some horses have cowlicks or retain longer hair in places even with their summer coat. Shaggy spots often appear around the chestnuts, on the upper leg, elbow, under the belly or on the throatlatch.

The head receives the most attention when clipping, and there are a multitude of ways to go about it. Minimal clipping of the face entails clipping with the 40 blade the whiskers and the long, whiskerlike hairs above and below the eyes, but many grooms clip far more than this.

In clipping the face, you want to enhance the horse's natural characteristics. Notice how the hair thins around the eyes and nose, allowing the black skin beneath to show through. Some horses naturally have a nice amount of the dark skin showing through in these areas, and this contributes to the beauty of the face. As part of grooming, you will remove the hair around the eyes and on the nose to let the dark

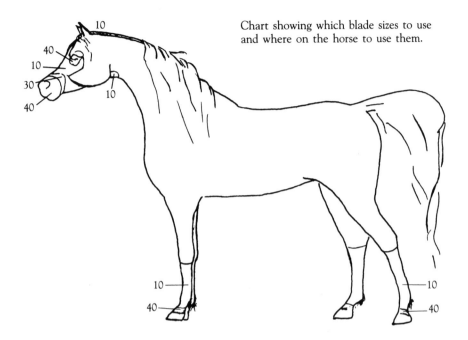

Chart showing which blade sizes to use and where on the horse to use them.

skin beneath show through. This is the only legal way to "darken" the areas around the eyes and nose because it is against horse show rules to use any pigments to artificially darken them.

Using the 40 blade, clip the whiskers from the nose and clip the hair from inside the nostrils (see page 129). On each side of the nose, remove the hair upward a short distance toward the tear bone. Use the 40 until you near the tear bone, then switch to 30 and go a bit farther. The goal is for this to look natural, as if no clippers have been used at all. The areas you clip should blend smoothly into the surrounding area. Remove the hair under the chin and on the front of the nose with the 40. Some bay or black horses have a light tan "mule look" around the nose. These horses look better if that light hair is removed completely. The 40 blade is not fine enough to do this. A smaller clipper made especially for clipping the ears works, or you can buy a man's disposable razor and use it to remove the hair. When you finish shaving, go back to the 40 blade and blend the shaved area into the hair above.

Beneath and above the eyes, use the 15 blade lightly to thin the hair

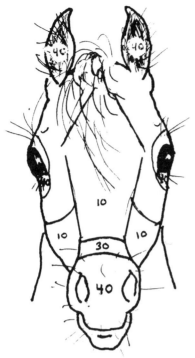

Blade sizes to use and where on the face to use them.

in a roughly triangular shape. Remove the long eyebrow hairs and the long stiff hairs beneath the eye.

If all of this shaving around the nose and eyes is well done, it will enhance the appearance of the horse's face. When done poorly and not blended well, the horse may look more like a raccoon. It's better to simply cut off the whiskers than make your horse look like a large woodland creature. For practice, work on the horses standing out in your pasture before you start grooming your show horse.

To thin the hair on the face, take the 10 or 15 blade and shave against the hair from in front of the jaw to the nose, then up the face. When you get to the level of the eyes, follow the inverted **V**-shape made by the bone of the horse's face. Carefully blend the **V** into the surrounding hair. With the 10 blade, remove any wispy hairs around the forelock. Also with the 10, shave between the jaws and remove any stray hairs on the jaw.

The head now is complete except for the ears and bridle path. Special clippers are available for clipping the ears. They are smaller and have a finer blade, and therefore tend to do a slightly better job (see page 130). However, regular clippers with a 40 blade also work well.

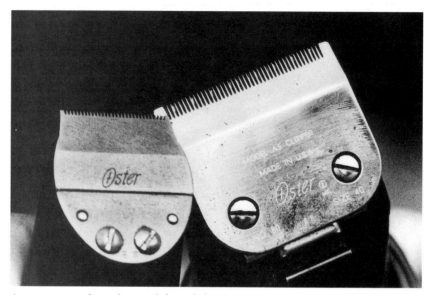

A comparison of ear clippers, left, and the size 40 clipper blades, right.

Clip all of the hair from the inside of the ear, except for a diamond-shaped patch at the tip of each ear. Also clip along the front and exterior rim of the ear, all the way around. If the diamond left at the tip is extremely fuzzy, trim a little of its surface. With the 10 blade, remove any long hairs from the exterior of the ears.

It is likely the horse will object to having his ears clipped. Some can be taught to tolerate it. Most have to be restrained in some manner. You may have to use a twitch or run a chain under the horse's upper lip. It might also help to tie a string to a cotton ball and put the cotton into the horse's ear. The cotton will muffle the sound and keep the clippings from falling inside. The string makes it easier to remove the cotton.

The 40 blade is used on the bridle path. The bridle path extends back from the bony protrusion that can be felt between the ears. The length is dictated by aesthetics. Some owners opt not to have bridle paths at all. Most bridle paths extend far enough back to clear the throatlatch. A thick-necked horse will look better if the bridle path is extended back farther. It tends to give the neck a more slim look.

# DEALING WITH SHAGGY BODY HAIR

The length of the day tells the horse when to grow a winter coat and when to shed it. The horse's body cares not at all that show season is fast approaching and you are desperately trying to get him to shed in time.

Blankets heaped upon the horse and a boost of the temperature in the barn do have some effect. They encourage the horse to grow a shorter winter coat and shed earlier. Proper nutrition will also aid in the growth of a good coat and in proper shedding. However, the main determinant is daylight. Increased amounts of daylight stimulate glands in the brain. The hair follicles are boosted into action and the horse sheds.

By using artificial light, you can induce the horse to shed early. To do this right, you will probably have to use timers to keep the barn lights on several hours after sunset. The lights must be used carefully and consistently. You are tampering with the horse's inner clock. If you forget to turn the lights on or off at the right time, suddenly it's winter again for the horse. You might confuse his body, making him hold onto that winter hair even longer.

Some people give their horses a small dose of strychnine to induce early shedding. It is toxic to quickly growing cells such as those found in the skin. It shocks the hair follicles and thus speeds shedding. While it may be effective, it is potentially dangerous and is not worth the risk.

If the hair absolutely must come off, a better course is to body-clip the horse. Some people body clip their horses every winter as a matter of routine. A horse that is body clipped will not sweat as heavily when worked, and will cool and dry faster. A body clip entails clipping, against the hair with a 10 blade, the entire body, from fetlock to the tip of the nose. It takes hours, and you may dull several 10 blades in the process. Long hair is left in two areas: in a small inverted **V** above the tail and, for the comfort of the horse, on the back. The area on the back should be cut to the size and shape of the saddle pad. Otherwise, the clipped hair under the saddle would feel bristly and encourage the horse to buck.

If you body-clip the horse while the weather is still cold, cover him with a blanket when he's not working. Nature put the shaggy hair there to keep him warm. If you remove it, the horse is going to need something to take its place.

# GROOMING

It is fairly common to spend an hour or more clipping and grooming a horse for the show ring. At-the-show preparations will be shortened and streamlined if you do most of the clipping while still at home. The horse then will just need grooming and a quick trim of the whiskers before going into the ring.

Grooming supplies vary from barn to barn, but a typical grooming box will include:

A mat or piece of carpet on which to work
Clippers with blades ranging from 10 to 40
Soft body brushes
Mane and tail brush
Towels
Petroleum jelly
Light oil
VO-5 or similar dressing
Sunscreen
Brilliantine
Fly spray
Coat dressing
Hair polish
Shoe polish, black, brown or neutral
Sandpaper, fine and medium
Electric sander
Steel wool, very fine (oo) or extra fine (ooo)
Hoof black, brown or neutral
Acrylic spray
Polish dryer
Twitch
A roll of paper towels

Bath supplies:
  Animal shampoo
  Sweat scraper
  Bucket
  Some type of scrubber
  Sponge
  Hose
  Cooler

The first step in grooming is to wash the horse. Any type of shampoo will do, but those designed for use on animals are better because they will not irritate the skin if soap remains on the horse's skin. Special soaps containing bluing are available for gray or white horses.

After rinsing the horse and scraping off the excess water, spray his entire body except for the saddle area with a hair polish that is not oil based. Hair polish will enhance the shine of the coat, make the mane and tail easier to comb and make it easier to remove any manure stains the horse may get after the bath.

Oil-based sprays attract dust. It is better to use them during the final grooming before the class, otherwise the horse may get dirty just standing in his stall.

After the horse dries, you can begin to work on the feet. The grooming process will be much easier if you have a clean surface on which to work. One of the easiest things to use is a large rubber mat or a piece of carpet turned upside down.

Sand the hooves first with medium-grade sandpaper, then fine-grade sandpaper, then steel wool until the surface feels like glass. The first time you sand the feet, it may take quite some time, depending on the roughness of the hooves. A power sander is often used to save time, but be careful not to burn the skin above the hoof or to sand the hoof down too far.

Once the surface of the hoof is smooth, apply a coating of shoe polish and then buff it. The color of the polish should correspond to the color of the hoof. The shoe polish will make the surface even smoother. On top of the buffed shoe polish, apply hoof polish that matches the color of the hoof. Use neutral on striped hoofs. It is illegal to use a polish that does not match the color of the hooves.

Polish can be water based or oil based. The latter tends to be shinier. When you are done with the hooves, they should look like patent leather (see below). If you want to dry the hooves in a hurry, polish dryer can be used. This is an aerosol product used by women to dry their fingernail polish quickly. It is available in most pharmacies and works just as well on hooves as fingernails. Sometimes the dryer dulls the shine slightly, but if you've got an impatient horse or need the hooves dry immediately, it's worth the tradeoff. An electric hair dryer like you use on your own hair can also be useful for drying hoofs, and hair, too, on those cool days.

Wait until the hooves dry before you do anything else to the horse. Wet hoof polish is sticky. If you brush the horse, you're likely to have hair stuck to the hooves.

After the hooves are done, go to work on the body. With a soft brush, go over the horse, head to foot. You can apply an oil-based hair polish now. If it is fly season, also put on some fly spray, especially on the legs and belly.

With a towel, wipe beneath the tail. Some grooms also oil this area. Comb out the mane and tail, then put on some hair polish or brilliantine (see page 135). Brilliantine is a product made for human hair and

A well-groomed hoof should shine like patent leather.

can be bought at a pharmacy. It will add gloss to the mane and tail. After the tail is done, if it is extremely long or if the ground is muddy, you may want to tie it up until it's time to go into the ring.

Once you're done with the body, you can begin work on the face. The face should be done last, since the oil and petroleum jelly you use there will attract dust. Some of the oil may also be absorbed into the skin.

Clean the face and interior of the ears. Inside the ears apply a light type of oil, VO-5 or a similar dressing. There are a number of these dressings, both those made for people and horses. Baby oil can be used, but there are lighter types of oil and cream dressings available. The lighter the oil or dressing, the better. You won't have as much of a problem with the dust sticking to it.

The VO-5, oil or dressing should also be massaged into the bridle path. Rub oil or dressing around and below the eyes, and on the nose and up the sides of it where the hair is thin. With the residue remaining

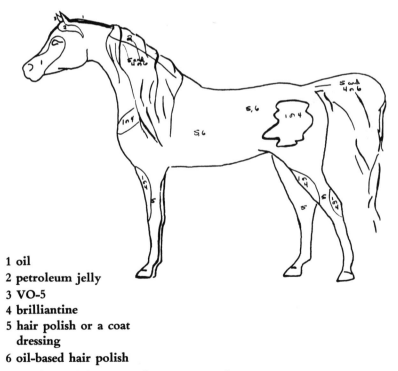

1 oil
2 petroleum jelly
3 VO-5
4 brilliantine
5 hair polish or a coat
  dressing
6 oil-based hair polish

Chart showing where to apply grooming supplies.

To put the tail up into a braid, you will need three strands of string or ribbon tied together at one end, a brush or comb and a vet wrap. To begin, divide the tail into three parts and braid them together, working in a ribbon with each strand. The braid should be loose around the tail bone, so it doesn't damage it. Braid the tail down to the end. (If it is fly season, divide the tail into four parts. Work the three parts into the braid, leaving the fourth free to swat flies.)

Loop the end of the tail through the braid at the top. Depending on the length of the tail, you may want to loop it through several times, doubling it over into a nice package.

on your hands, lightly brush the rest of the horse's face.

If the day is hot and sunny, and the horse is not used to that much sun, you may want to put a strong sunscreen around his eyes and nose, particularly if they are pink. Horses can get painful sunburns at some of the midsummer outdoor shows. The oil placed on the nose and eyes makes the horse even more prone to burn. For the sunny shows, use an oil-based sunscreen instead. The sunscreen should be at least number 15, and is the same type you would use on yourself. Be careful not to get the sunscreen in the horse's eyes. Should the horse get a sunburn, the sunburn preparations that feel good to you will feel good to him, too, especially aloe vera preparations.

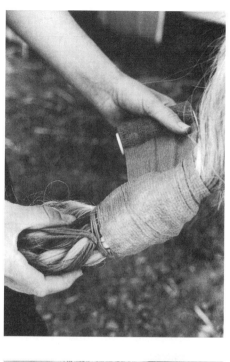

(Below.) When you have finished looping the end of the tail through, take the ribbon or string dangling from the end of the tail and tie it around the package of hair.

(Top right.) Wrap the vet wrap around the package of hair.

(Right.) A finished wrap.

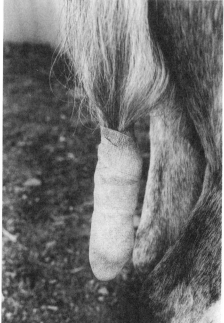

The petroleum jelly is used to thoroughly coat the forelock from roots to tip. This will help hold the forelock when it is pulled to the side and tucked beneath the bridle. (It is illegal to show with the mane or tail braided, except in hunter-type classes.) Also apply the jelly across the crest of the mane to hold down any short, wispy hairs.

# BETWEEN-SHOW GROOMING

For the horse to look good at the show, he has to receive the proper care at home. Proper nutrition and exercise are essential for his health and the shine of his coat. Weather permitting, cover him with a light sheet when he goes outside. This will help keep the flies from bothering him and will minimize sun damage to its coat. Sun damage makes the hair look reddish and fuzzy.

Frequent brushing, which works the body oils through the hair, makes the coat shiny. Massaging light oil into the hair also promotes coat health.

The hooves also must be cared for. After each show, use rubbing alcohol to strip off the hoof polish. Then moisturize the hooves with one of the hoof preparations on the market. Barn horses in particular need this treatment. They rarely have the benefit of standing in mud, which moisturizes the pasture horse's hooves. Some types of bedding can also draw moisture from the hooves.

Long manes and tails are part of the elegance of the breed. Between shows, you may want to put up both the mane and the tail. The mane and forelock can be braided into pony tails, with the number depending on how thick the mane is. When the pony tails become frayed-looking, take them down and rebraid them. If the horse is in a pasture where he can catch his mane on snags, it is better to leave the mane unbraided.

The tail can be braided as well (see pages 136 and 137). Braiding helps the tail grow long and thick by preventing damage to the hair from weather, swatting at flies, or getting snagged on objects or stepped on.

If the horse has a nice thick tail, leave a swatch of it out of the braid, to give the horse something to drive away flies with.

# 13

# Hauling

YOUR HORSE IS GOING TO spend many hours in horse trailers whisking along the continent's highways. With a little work and forethought, you can help make those trips easier on him.

## TEACHING THE HORSE TO HAUL

There is no specific age when a horse should be taught to load and haul. Often a foal will get his first ride beside the comforting presence of his mother when she returns to the stallion to be rebred. Unless the foal continues to be hauled, don't expect that first ride will make him an expert hauler. Learning to haul takes a little practice, which should be stress free and short. Once he accepts the experience, he'll probably haul easily for the rest of his life unless something happens to shake his confidence.

Some large farms and hauling companies use semi-trailer vans to transport horses, while most people use some type of horse trailer (see below). If you have a semi instead of a horse trailer, you'll probably have an easier time of loading and hauling your horse. Semi vans are more open, and some horses accept them more readily. It's a good thing, too, since the size of the van makes it hard to take the novice horse out for a few short rides to get him used to hauling. His first ride is likely to be a genuine trip instead of practice.

A standard trailer.

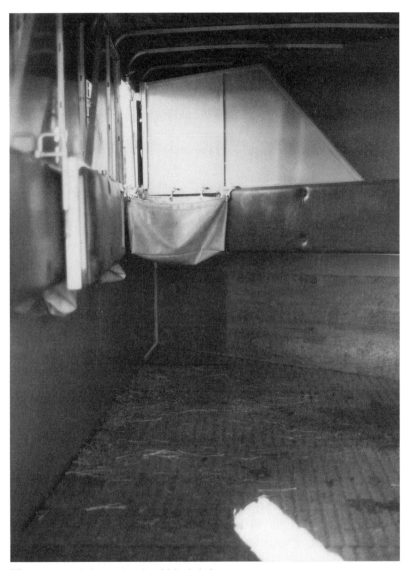

The interior of the trailer should look light.

Trailers are often difficult at first for the novice horse, perhaps because they are more confining than semis. Before loading the horse, open any small windows to make the interior look lighter and more spacious, but don't open any large windows or doors or the horse might try to bolt through them if he becomes frightened.

Before attempting to load the horse, be sure the trailer is hooked to the truck, otherwise it could move when the horse enters.

Lead the horse up to the trailer. Then step inside the trailer and, with small tugs on the rope, urge him to follow. You may want to use food as a bribe. If he enters a few steps, then backs out, don't try to restrain him the first few times. He's building courage, testing to see if it's safe. When he seems a little more confident, don't allow him to back out. Urge him all the way in, then fasten the butt chain.

Many horses will actually walk into the trailer the first time without much effort, but you should devise loading methods to suit the situation and the personality of the horse.

If you cannot get the horse into the trailer with gentle persuasion, tap him gently on the rump with the whip to encourage him inside. Don't hit him hard enough to cause pain. You're trying to impress upon him that hauling is no big deal. You don't want the horse associate the trailer with fear and pain. He could become so stubborn, angry or confused that his mind will shut down from the stress. If that happens, you could have a considerable fight on your hands—one you probably could have avoided with a little patience. Striking the novice horse is a last resort.

If you cannot persuade the horse to enter, you might try another tack. Urge the horse up to the entrance of the trailer, then have two strong people put their shoulders to his rump and literally shove him inside. If you can get the horse to lean forward into the trailer a little, or the people are the type that you might see on Prime Time Wrestling, this method will work even with large horses. It throws the horse off balance, and he stumbles inside. But the method has to work the first or second time. The horse quickly gets wise to it and will sit down on your assistants the moment he feels pressure from the rear.

Once he is inside, fasten the butt chain and let him stand there for a few minutes. The chain will keep him from backing out. Provide food for him to munch on to give the impression that being in the trailer is not all that bad. For his first experience, if it's a fairly roomy trailer and he is not agitated, you could stand in there with him while the trailer is stationary. If you do not stay with him, tie him up inside the trailer.

The length of the rope you use depends on the height of the horse and where the ties are located in the trailer. If he can reach his head down below his chest, the rope is too long. If he can scarcely move his head from side to side and up and down, it's too short. The horse will dectate the length. If he pulls back, he may be telling you the rope is too short. If he moves around excessively in the trailer, he may have too much rope. The attachment he is tied to should be at or above eye level.

If the horse seems to be accepting his first experience with the trailer well, take him for a short drive. This is for your peace of mind as much as to get him used to traveling. If the first time you haul him is to a show, you can't be certain of his condition when you get there. The horse probably would be fine, but you might open the trailer doors to find him wild-eyed, trembling and soaked in a cold sweat. You could also find that he panicked on the way and injured himself. Such things happen, and if it is going to happen at all, it is better to be close to home and not at the big show you've waited all year to attend.

After a few short rides, most horses will accept the hauling experience. At first your horse may move around in the trailer quite a bit or paw or kick, especially when the trailer has stopped or slowed down. These actions will fade when he has more experience. By the end of the first show season, he'll be a veteran hauler. If a horse that hauls well begins to stomp or paw or exhibit other signs of agitation unusual for him, stop the trailer and check on him. Something could be wrong. He may just be hot, or it might be something serious.

As the horse becomes more experienced, if possible discontinue the practice of entering the trailer with him. While it appears the easiest way to get the novice horse into a trailer, it is not a safe practice. It is safer if you train the horse to go into the trailer alone. Horse trailers have escape doors through which you can exit, but when a horse panics inside a trailer there may not be time to get out, and you could get hurt.

## THE VETERAN HAULER

The veteran knows what trailers and hauling are all about. Despite this, or maybe because of it, he will occasionally refuse to enter the trailer. If it is a trailer he is unaccustomed to, use a little patience. Tug on the rope and tap him with the whip. If it is the same type of trailer he's always hauled in, he's being obnoxious by refusing to enter. Be a little more strict with him. Use the form of persuasion he will respond to best. Some horses respond to the whip. Others respond better to tension on that chain. They step forward into the trailer to relieve the tension. Extreme force is not necessary. Hitting the horse repeatedly is no more effective than hitting him once or twice. Threatening to hit him may be just as effective as actually hitting him. It shouldn't take very much to get the veteran in. Loosing your temper is useless, foolish and can lead to abuse of the horse.

A horse that is injured in a trailer or involved in an accident may develop a fear of hauling. Pounding on him to get him into the trailer will not help matters any. His fear of the trailer may be greater than that of the whip or chain. To help him over his fear, you may have to start teaching him to haul all over again, as if he were a novice.

## COMFORT AND SAFETY IN THE TRAILER

On some trips the horse may have to spend all day or several days in the trailer or van. There are some things you can do to make him more comfortable so he will arrive at your destination less tired.

Shipping boots (see page 145) protect the legs and come in various lengths. You can also protect the legs with a layer of sheet cotton or disposable diapers, over which are placed standard leg wraps. Helmets to protect the horse's head are also available. Whatever you use, try them out on the horse and let him to get used to them before hauling him. Because he has worn a variety of other tack, he'll probably only need to walk around in the wraps and helmet for a few minutes to get used to them.

If the horse is being hauled long distances with other horses, make sure his vaccinations are current. Trailers and vans are prime sites for horses to pick up illnesses because of the close quarters. The stress of the trip also may lower the horse's ability to fight off illness. While vaccinations will not protect the horse from colds, they may keep him from getting something more serious.

For the safety and comfort of the horse, cover the floor of the trailer

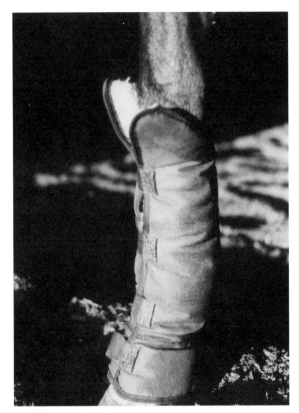

Standard horse shipping boots.

or van with thick rubber mats. This gives the horse better traction. Manure and urine can make a wooden trailer floor quite slick. Mats also help absorb concussion and make the ride easier on the legs. On top of the mats you may want a layer of coarse shavings to help with the footing and absorb urine. Without the shavings the horse may be reluctant to urinate because the urine will splash on his legs. Avoid using fine sawdust on the floor because it may blow around inside the trailer.

Be conscious of the temperature inside the trailer. If it is hot, open the trailer vents. If is cold, blanket the horse. Stop occasionally to check on how the horse is doing, or if you sense unusual activity in the trailer, such as a lot of scrambling and banging.

Hay will keep the horse entertained for a while as the miles go by. The hay should be as clean and dust free as possible, since in the close confines of the trailer dust is more likely to cause respiratory disturbances in the horse. If you are feeding in a hay bag, make sure you tie it high enough so the horse cannot get his legs tangled in it. Do not feed the horse anything that could possibly get caught in his throat, such as apples, while he is riding in the trailer.

If possible arrange stopovers on long journeys, so the horse can be boarded overnight. Trips are physically and mentally taxing, especially in trailers. Vans have a little more room, and it is common for horses to spend the night in them on long trips.

If the horse is injured while in transit, if at all possible leave him in the trailer unless there is a better option available. Some factors to consider:

- How bad is the injury? This is going to be very difficult to tell with the horse in the trailer, but in this kind of an emergency you only need to determine the following: (1) Is it obviously minor, so you can treat the horse then continue the trip? (2) Does the injury appear serious enough to need veterinary attention? Does it appear life-threatening? If you cannot tell how bad the injury is, call a vet just in case it is more serious than it appears. Your need for a vet is urgent if blood is spurting from a wound, the horse appears to be going into shock or something appears to be broken. Do what you can to get the bleeding stopped and the horse stabilized, but call the vet or send someone for a vet first. Every second counts.
- Does the risk of unloading the horse outweigh the risk of leaving him in the trailer? Unloading the horse is your very last resort. It's likely that, if you discover the injury before reaching your destination, you'll be at a gas station or rest stop along the roadside or at some other less-than-ideal place for coping with something like this. The trailer may be your only way to get the horse to medical help. You may have to haul the horse to a vet or drive to a phone and call for help.

The injured horse will be frightened, particularly of the trailer in which he was hurt. If you unload him, you run the risk of not being able to get him back into the trailer. Only unload him if the risk of leaving him in the trailer outweighs the risk of removing him. If you do have to unload him, try to find a place where you will have room to work and not be in danger of traffic. While you work on the horse, send anyone you can recruit to get a veterinarian.

- What is the fastest way of getting veterinary help for the horse? You have three options: (1) send someone to find a vet while you work on the horse; (2) call a veterinarian to come to you; or (3) get directions to the vet's office, then haul the horse there. The last two options are the fastest.

## THE HORSE TRAILER

The most important element for the safety and comfort of the horse is the trailer itself. The type of trailer you use will depend on the number of horses you have to haul and how large a tack room you want in it.

Ideally, the trailer should be structurally sound, particularly in the floorboards, and large enough to give the horse a little room to move around. There should be no sharp points or edges in the interior, and no spaces the horse possibly could get his leg through. Check for anything that could come loose or cut the horse or entangle him. Don't be fooled into thinking the horse couldn't possibly reach a problem area you have spotted in the trailer. He will be spending a lot of time there unsupervised, and practically anything can happen. He can surprise you in very unpleasant ways.

And don't think that just because the trailer was safe for the last horse, it will be for the next. Trailers age. Parts can rattle loose. Wooden floorboards can rot. Be on the lookout for safety hazards in the trailer. Lift up the rubber mats on the floor and check the floorboards. If the trailer has a manger, feel around it for sharp edges or points that may have been exposed as the padding wears. Check the walls and ceiling for protruding bolts or other safety problems.

Before leaving on any trip, check the brakes and trailer lights. Make sure the trailer is hitched properly, and to the right hitch and a mechanically sound towing vehicle. If you have had problems with the trailer swaying, you may want to have sway bars or another stabilizing device on the hitch. Check the tires for wear and be sure they are properly inflated. Always carry a spare tire and a jack that is stout enough to lift the trailer.

If you are crossing state lines, make sure your papers for horses are in order. Contact the Department of Agriculture of the state you are visiting to see what is required to enter that state. You may need a certificate from the brand inspector in your home state. Some states also require specific health tests.

# PROFESSIONAL HAULING SERVICES

The horse may spend hours on the road, but you do not have to. There are many good hauling services that will transport horses practically anywhere in the United States and Canada. They charge on a per-mile basis. When you have to transport a horse over a great distance, you may find it easier to use one of these services rather than haul the horse yourself.

Hauling services are used for a variety of reasons: to bring home horses that have been bought in distant places, to transport mares to or from the breeding barn or to drop off horses to be sold. If you are looking for a transportation company, check it out carefully. Select an established business, one that has a good reputation among fellow horse enthusiasts, with a good safety record and facilities that meet with your approval for the safety and comfort of your horse.

# 14

# Conditioning

THE GREATEST GIFT YOU CAN give your horse to ensure continued good performance, health and soundness is to keep him in excellent physical condition. A horse that is out of shape risks being injured, experiences greater stress and tires easily during long shows, all of which make it harder for him to be at his best.

Conditioning produces physical changes that strengthen and increase the efficiency of the horse's body. He becomes less prone to injury, more willing and able to perform and healthier. Conditioning him takes work, but the rewards far outweigh the effort.

As the horse exercises, protein slowly builds in the muscle fibers, making them thicker and stronger. More energy reserves are packed into the fibers as well, and the fibers become more efficient in their ability to convert nutrients to energy. As his fitness level rises, the supply of blood to the muscles improves. Increased blood provides an increased supply of oxygen to the muscles.

Conditioning makes the heart muscle stronger, enabling it to beat faster longer and increasing the volume of blood it can pump per heart beat. A horse that is in shape can work harder but tax his heart less than the equine version of a couch potato. The increased efficiency of the heart enables the fit horse to recover faster from a hard workout.

The entire circulatory system is improved by exercise. New capillaries form to feed the muscles and carry away waste more effectively. The network of capillaries around the lungs expands, allowing carbon dioxide to be eliminated and oxygen picked up faster and in greater volume. The expanding blood supply here and in the skin will help the horse throw off more heat during exertion, which is one of the reasons the fit horse does not sweat as heavily as the flabby horse.

To further improve the oxygen delivery system, exercise encourages the body to produce more red blood cells, the oxygen-carrying agents of the blood. To improve their endurance, human athletes sometimes have transfusions of red blood cells before a competition, giving their body more oxygen-carrying agents. The fit body strives to do the same thing—produce more red blood cells to improve endurance.

Conditioning brings physical changes to the entire body, including the bones. As the bones undergo stress, they become increasingly dense in the areas stressed. Areas of the bone not stressed lose density. The strengthening of bone occurs faster in younger horses than those that have matured.

The conditioning program you design for you horse should take all of these changes into consideration as you seek to remodel his body to the optimum for the task you will ask him to perform. Because muscles and bones only grow stronger when used, the basis of the conditioning program will be the same work you ask of him in the ring.

The conditioning given a stock horse differs from that given an English horse. Each requires strength in different areas for different purposes. For example, the sliding stop performed by the stock horse takes a great deal of muscle and bone strength in the hindquarters. The hind legs of a stock horse often appear very muscular. An English horse also must have a strong hindquarters, but the muscle development and requirements for bone strength differ.

There is no "quick" way to condition a horse, no quick-fix programs for horses. Fast conditioning programs don't work any better for horses than they do for people.

The length of time it will take for the horse to reach an adequate level of endurance and strength will depend on a number of factors. A horse that has taken a four-month vacation will be easier to get back in shape than one that has scarcely had any exercise for a year. Just as exercise produces changes in the body, so does idleness. Muscles weaken and grow thinner as the protein content in them drops. Bones lose strength as well. Cardiovascular efficiency lessens. If the horse has had some exercise during his vacation, these changes will occur at a slower rate, and thus he will shape up faster because his body has not lost as much conditioning.

The horse's weight, activity levels and environment also have a bearing on conditioning. A horse that is obese will take longer to condition than one that is flabby but within reasonable weight ranges. A horse that is active on his own is easier to condition because he tends to keep himself in better shape. A horse given time off in a pasture tends to stay more fit than the horse in a stall because the pasture horse has a greater opportunity for exercise.

The moral is that a little exercise during the off season will make it easier to get the horse in shape when show season comes. Adjust the food you give him according to the amount of work he is doing. He should be getting less when he is not working. Obesity is unbecoming in a performance horse. A little fat is encouraged in halter horses, but not in performance horses. Leaner horses will work better and be healthier.

Fat burdens the horse's systems (see page 152). The muscles, lungs and cardiovascular system must work harder. The muscle has more bulk to move, the lungs must work against the weight and provide more oxygen for the additional tissue and the heart must work harder. Increased weight from fat causes more concussion on the legs, straining bones, ligaments and tendons. Fat horses are also more prone to founder.

Athletes are lean and muscular, whether they are human or horses. You probably will never see a successful fat racehorse. Fat hampers athletic ability.

The level of fitness you condition the horse for will depend on the

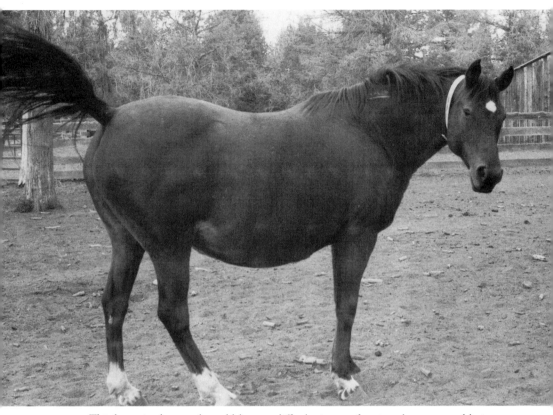

This horse is obese and would have a difficult time performing almost any athletic task.

task he will be asked to perform. An English horse expected to go in one class a day at a show does not have to be as fit as an endurance horse, but still must be in good shape. You may not think it takes much fitness to successfully complete a fifteen- to twenty-minute class, but for each of those minutes the horse must give his all. He must be collected and brilliant. It takes stamina and strength for him to be able to perform well and consistently class after class.

The fit horse also has a little bit more to offer. His limits have been pushed farther back. Tasks become easier for him, and he is more likely to enjoy the physical effort. As any person who has stuck to a fitness routine can testify, the better shape you are in, the more physical activities you want to perform.

It takes around three months to get a horse in adequate condition, again depending on the original condition of the horse and the fitness level he must reach. It can take six months or more of conditioning for him to reach optimum fitness. Don't confuse getting the horse to his ideal weight with getting him in shape. A horse can look lean and still lack good muscle tone. Feel his legs, shoulders, withers, barrel and rump. Muscle feels hard. Fat feels squishy. As the horse's condition improves, his underline will become less rounded. He will become firmer, and your fingers will no longer make much more than a slight indentation when you press on his shoulders or back. Probably the last areas he will firm will be in the rump and the fatty strip extending down from his withers.

How much the horse sweats during a workout is questionable as an indicator of condition or even how hard he is working. While a conditioned horse will sweat less, sweating is also influenced by weather and stress.

A more accurate way to track his improving physical condition is through his heart rate. Check his resting heart rate several times to establish a baseline rate. You can take the pulse by pressing your fingers into the artery at the inside of the jaw (see page 154). To establish a working heart rate, trot or canter him at a brisk, consistent speed for five minutes, then take his pulse. Then walk him for five minutes, and take his pulse again. Do this every week, and record your findings. As his condition improves, you'll find that his resting and working heart rates will slow as his cardiovascular system improves in efficiency. You'll also find he recovers faster after work.

Start the conditioning program slowly. Take care not to work the horse to exhaustion. That is when injuries occur. Begin each workout with a warmup period consisting of walking and a mild trot. If you are riding, add to this some small circles to flex his neck and back to each side. The warmup will give his body a chance to prepare for work. Blood will shift to the muscles, and the muscles will warm and become more limber. This staves off strain and injury. Warmup also serves as a mental preparation. Five minutes before you removed him from his stall, he may have been taking a nap. Now he needs to be alert and concentrate on your demands.

Warmup time will vary from horse to horse, but ten minutes is usually sufficient. This is just the time it takes to warm the body. The

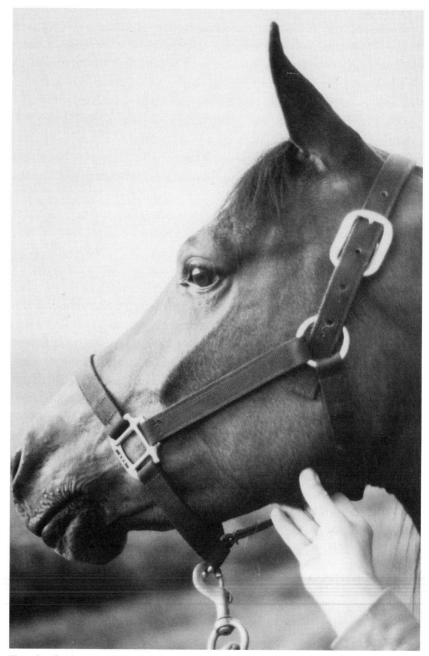

To take the horse's pulse, feel for the artery at the inside of the jawbone.

horse may be well into the workout before he begins to work to his optimum.

For the first two to three weeks of the conditioning program, a half hour workout will be sufficient, again depending on the horse's original condition. Within each workout, the English horse should be walked, trotted and cantered. Emphasis should be on a collected trot. Not only is it the focal point of an English horse, it also tends to demand more physical exertion, so is the most beneficial to a conditioning program.

Most of the conditioning probably will take place under saddle. When ridden, the horse will work harder because you are pushing him and making him stay collected. Riding is also vastly more interesting for you than standing in the middle of a circle watching him lunge for what can seem like an eternity.

Most trainers do not ride the same horse every day, especially if the horse is seasoned. On days the horse is not ridden, he still should be exercised. In a good conditioning program, the horse is exercised five to six days a week. On the days he is not ridden he should be lunged, long lined or worked free. Lungeing involves the handler's working the horse in a circle at the trot and canter. The horse may be wearing only a halter, or he may be bitted up—wearing a bridle with the reins tied back to the saddle or a surcingle in order to keep his head set in the desired position.

While lungeing and long lining are good exercise, the small circles the horse is worked in tend to put a strain on the inside legs, especially the inside foreleg. Lungeing him free in an arena is less of a strain because the horse is not performing in small circles, and this also gives him more opportunity to play and enjoy himself.

At first you may have little or no control over the gaits of the free horse. During the first few workouts, the thrill of being loose may encourage him to run and buck for much of the time. As he becomes accustomed to this form of exercise and learns that these workouts last for quite some time, he will relax and may pay more attention to voice commands. This is especially true of horses that have been worked on the lunge line. Some tend to work free, as though the line was still there, and do not notice that you really do not have any control over them. Free lungeing works best in a mid-sized arena. If you pick one that is too large, you'll be the one getting the workout as you run from one end to the other trying to keep the horse going.

Work the horse at the trot and canter, providing as many walking breaks as he needs to recover. This should be done when lungeing and long lining the horse as well. At first he may need a walking break every fifteen minutes. As his condition improves and the workouts become longer, he will need the walking breaks less frequently. Don't let him stand still while he is catching his breath in the middle of a hard workout, especially if he is really hot.

When working the horse free, you will have to catch and lead him at the walk to prevent him from standing while he is catching his breath. If the horse tends to start his free workout too strong, you may want to start him out on the lunge line for a warmup at a mild trot. The warmup will lessen his chance of injury.

Most horses learn to free-lunge rapidly. Some, however, do not learn moderation, and nearly every time will run until they are foaming with sweat and gasping for air. Others will buck and put themselves through contortions they do not have the physical coordination for. This happens mostly with young horses, and since these horses are likely to injure themselves, they should be exercised under more controlled situations until they can handle loose exercise.

Some horse farms have yet another equine exercise option available to them—swimming. While installing an equine swimming pool is expensive, swimming offers the building of muscle without concussion to the legs. It is excellent for horses that have suffered injuries because it maintains fitness without further stressing the injury.

It does, however, have its drawbacks. It should not become the only source of exercise for a healthy horse. The horse needs a certain amount of concussion to his legs in order for the bones to remain strong. If swimming is not combined with ground exercise, the horse may become more prone to concussion injuries.

While pools have yet to become commonplace, many barns do have treadmills. Treadmills work the horse at a slight incline, and often are used to condition halter horses.

After any type of exercise, walk the horse until he is cool. Failure to cool the horse may cause muscle cramps, muscle damage or colic. During exercise, the blood supply shifts to the muscles. If he returns

Overreach boots.

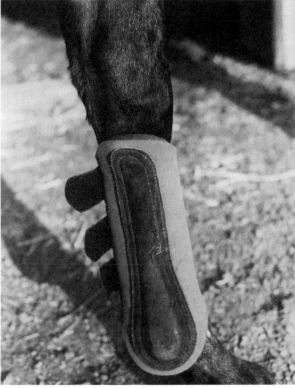

Splint boots.

to his stall and consumes a large amount of food and water while still hot, his digestive system will not have a sufficient supply of blood to handle it, and he may colic.

The length of time it takes to cool the horse will, of course, depend on how hard he has been worked and his physical condition. It probably will take at least fifteen minutes. After an extremely hard workout, he may need more time. He can be rinsed or sponged off to help the cooling process along. Icy-cold water should be avoided. If the water feels uncomfortably cold to your hands, it is far too cold for the horse.

When walking the horse, a cooler blanket will help cool at the proper rate. A cooler is particularly important if the weather is cold.

# PROTECTING THE LEGS

When the horse is worked or turned out, precautions should be taken to protect the legs. This is particularly important with young horses.

To wrap the leg with polo wraps: Lay the end of the wrap without the Velcro against the cannon bone, then begin wrapping down the leg.

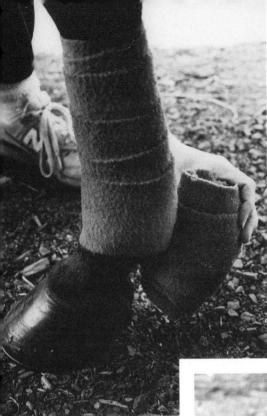

When pulling the wrap snug on the leg, pull toward the back of the leg, so the tension in the wrap goes across bone. Once you get across the bone, stop pulling as you bring the wrap back and around the tendons at the back of the leg. Then pull snugly again across the bone at the front of the leg. This will give you a nice snug wrap without disturbing the tendons. When you get to the fetlock, angle the wrap down toward the ground, then upward as you bring the wrap around the leg so the wrap covers the fetlock joint.

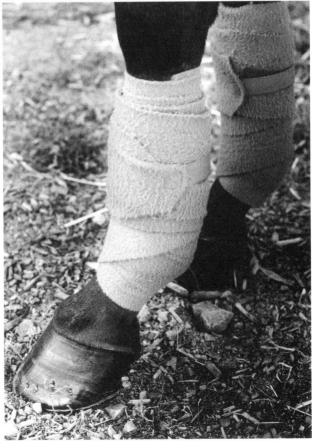

A finished wrap.

Most commonly used on English horses are bell boots (see page 157), splint boots (see page 157) and leg wraps. Bell boots are rubber boots that fit around the pasterns and protect the back of the feet. They shield the horse from bruises and cuts that occur when he interferes with his stride. The boots should fit around the pasterns slightly loose, but no so much so that they flop or rotate.

Splint boots lend some support to the legs from just below the knees down to the fetlock joints.

I prefer to use wraps instead of splint boots. Wrapping the leg with polo bandages, which are made from stretch fleece, allows greater flexibility in the area you want to protect. They can cover the same area as a splint boot and also extend down to provide more support to the fetlock joint itself (see pages 158 and 159).

Other devices used for leg protection include ankle boots for horses that hit their ankles when in motion, hock boots for the protection and support of the hocks and skid boots, which are used by stock and cutting horses for the protection of the rear fetlocks.

# 15

# Shoeing

SHOEING INFLUENCES THE HORSE'S WAY of going.

There are nearly as many types shoes for horses as there are for people. Golfers and joggers wear different shoes, and so do the English horse and the barrel racer. Shoeing should always be done by a farrier, but if you understand why English horses are shod the way they are, you can determine if your farrier is doing your horse justice.

Shoeing cannot create English motion in a horse that has none, nor can excellent shoeing overcome mediocrity. Arabians' shoes are not heavy enough to cause more than small improvements in gaits. The best horse will still win the class, even if its shoeing is ordinary. Proper shoeing can, however, enhance what motion the horse has.

Shoeing regulations, which are governed by the American Horse Shows Association, specify that Arabians are limited to hoof lengths of 4½ inches and shoe weights of 14 ounces (excluding nails). A single ⅜-inch leather or plastic full or rim pad between the shoe and hoof is permitted. The chains, rollers, layers of pads and other devices seen on other breeds, such as Saddlebreds, are not permitted. AHSA rules do change, so before each show season, check your new AHSA Rule Book for possible changes in shoeing regulations.

Fourteen ounces of weight and 4½ inches of hoof is not a lot for a farrier to work with to influence the motion of a thousand-pound animal. The weight of Saddlebred shoes can be more than six times that worn by Arabians. Even with lighter shoes, however, there are some things that commonly are done to enhance English motion.

There is no one correct way to shoe a horse for English. Horses are individuals. A formula used successfully on one horse may have a totally different effect on another. The farrier's job is to discover what works best for your horse.

The angles of a horse's body produce the leverage he needs to move. When the horse is shod, attention must be paid to those angles. The pastern and shoulder of a horse are at the same angle. The hoof should be, too. Some people deviate from this angle when having a horse shod. Too much deviation, however, can cause lameness. We must remember that a thousand-pound horse is standing on those four little hooves. What is done to the hooves will affect the well-being of the entire animal.

In general, most English horses are shod with the maximum shoe weight and maximum toe length allowed by the AHSA rules. The exception is green horses, because they may not have the coordination and maturity to work well at maximum shoe weight and maximum toe length. With mature horses, the shoe usually is designed to make the horse put more effort into the stride, with particular emphasis on breakover—the time when the toe lifts off the ground. The more effort exerted in breakover, the higher the stride. Some English horses will move better if breakover is made easier, but usually most move better if breakover is harder. Western horses are just the opposite—they tend to move better if breakover is easier.

In shoeing English horses, the emphasis is on the front hooves because to a certain extent you can enhance action up front. The hind hooves do not receive as much attention because the effect of rear shoeing is minimal. You cannot "manufacture" hock action.

Nearly all English horses are fitted with front shoes that have rolled toes (see page 163), which aid high knee action. Walking horses, however, rarely wear rolled toes because they are shod to cover ground quickly. They need a toe that will dig in and help them produce a ground-covering stride. The rolled toe favored for English horses works by *failing* to "dig in." As the hoof rocks forward, the rolled toe provides little purchase. The toe quickly snaps backward, creating a higher arc to the knee. This may be inefficient, but by the standards of the show ring, it is a better way of going. It is part of the look of the English horse.

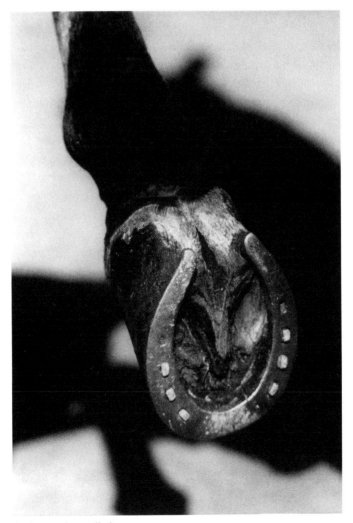

A shoe with a rolled toe.

The snapping backward of the toe begins the curling or folding of the pastern, then the knee, as the horse brings up his leg. The amount the leg curls plays a key role in how high the horse will trot and how much extension will be attained as the horse unfolds the leg to reach forward. In some horses, the leg will fold to the point the hoof nearly strikes the horse's elbow. Folding also may be aided by the distribution of the weight in the shoe. While the light shoes worn by Arabians do not give the farrier much to work with, shoes can be made so that much of the weight is contained in the front, middle or back of the shoe.

Where the weight will best contribute to the desired motion varies from breed to breed and from horse to horse. Weight in the toe of a Standardbred tends to make the horse throw his leg out straight, with very little folding taking place. Toe weights in many of the breeds used in English, such as Arabians, National Show Horses and Morgans, tend to increase the fold, making the horse trot higher.

In general, if the English horse is throwing his leg forward instead of curling, the weight in the toe may help. The farrier may want to experiment with the weight by tacking a pad and a lead weight to the hooves. The horse then can be ridden and his motion observed. Then the weight can be moved to a different area of the pad, and the exercise repeated until the best location for the weight is found. A shoe can be built accordingly. Sometimes it is a good sign when the horse goes much worse, because it is an indication that the opposite in shoeing might create a significant improvement.

English horses commonly are shod with the shoe extending slightly beyond the back of the hoof (see page 165). More of a protective measure than an effort to increase motion, it keeps the hoof from rocking back before breakover. Although the hoof rocking backward will force the horse to put more effort into the stride, thus producing more motion, it strains the tendons and suspensory ligaments in the leg. Lameness and problems such as bowed tendons can result.

How far the shoe should extend behind the front hoof depends on the horse. Some horses step on the extensions with their hind hooves, literally pulling off the front shoes. This is unlikely to occur with a well-trained, collected horse, but horses do not have riders on them twenty-four hours a day to keep them collected. The horse could pull the shoes off during play in a paddock. Shoeing the hind feet slightly

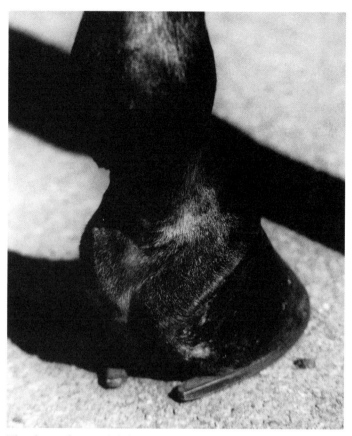

The shoes of an English horse are often extended back beyond the buttress of the hoof to protect the tendons and ligaments at the back of the leg.

shorter, and squaring the toe of the hind hooves, can help prevent this.

To find a good farrier, ask around. Who is working on the English horses in your area? Who is shoeing the horses at the major stables? It's likely they will hire some of the best farriers. The American Farriers Association keeps listings of certified journeymen farriers throughout the United States, and you may want to get names this way.

To evaluate the work of your farrier, consider how your horse is traveling. If you are happy, then the farrier is doing right by your horse. Keep a record listing the farrier used, when the horse was shod and the length of his hooves.

Watch the farrier work and look at the finished product. The frog should be a clean **V**-shape with all the diseased portions removed (see page 167). As much healthy tissue as possible should be retained.

The bars are extensions of the wall and should not be trimmed to the point they do not bear weight. Their shape may look like ramps, climbing upward from the level of the sole at the interior of the foot and getting higher toward the rear of the foot. If the farrier uses a slightly different treatment of the bars, they will appear more blended into the level of the sole. Either treatment is adequate.

As the bars reach back toward the heel, they should become even with the wall. If they protrude beyond that, bruising may result. Toward the inside of the hoof, the bars should not be trimmed below the level of the sole.

The amount of sole removed depends on how much excess growth accumulates and the kind of work the horse does. Usually some of the sole is removed in the toe area and blended into the toe wall. Dead sole, that flaky white matter in the hoof, is removed. The sole will be concave, dipping inward from the wall of the hoof.

The wall bears the horse's weight and is trimmed to keep weight distribution even. It should not look like all the weight is on the front or the rear of the hoof, or on one hoof more than another. The hooves should not be shod at lengths and at angles varying greatly from one another. Having hooves at different lengths and angles probably feels much to the horse as it does to you if you put on two different kinds of shoes and try to walk. It makes you move strangely and can do the same to the horse.

Flares and dishes in the hoof can be removed and the hoof reshaped somewhat. The upper two inches of the hoof wall dictate the angle to which the hoof should be trimmed. Often for corrective shoeing, the farrier will remove a little more from one area of the wall than another. This changes the natural movement of the horse. A horse that toes out, for example, can be shod to move straighter.

When it comes to English horses, however, it does not matter if the horse is moving with the strict correctness of a halter horse. In fact, if the horse lacks correctness, shoeing it to try to make it move straighter can detract from the English motion you wanted in the first place. "If it ain't broke, don't fix it" applies here as well. Unless the horse's conformation quirks are interfering with his ability to perform

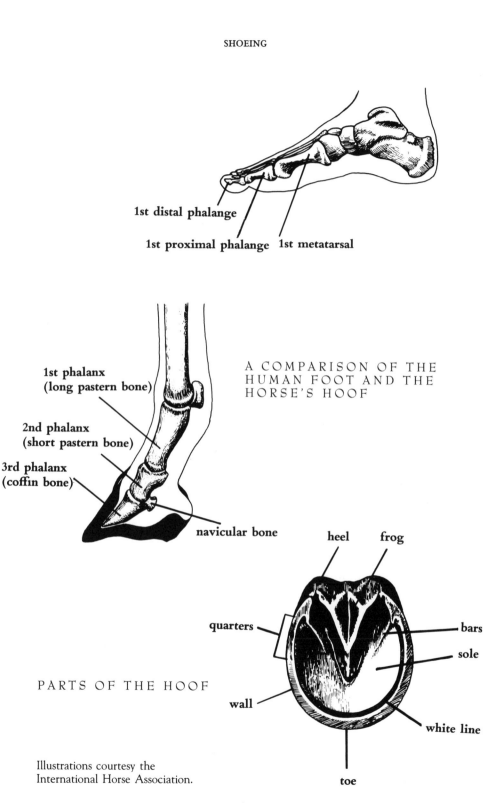

1st distal phalange

1st proximal phalange  1st metatarsal

A COMPARISON OF THE
HUMAN FOOT AND THE
HORSE'S HOOF

1st phalanx
(long pastern bone)

2nd phalanx
(short pastern bone)

3rd phalanx
(coffin bone)

navicular bone

heel    frog

quarters    bars

sole

PARTS OF THE HOOF

wall

white line

Illustrations courtesy the
International Horse Association.

toe

the gaits, don't try to fix him by pressing him into a mold of correct conformation. Don't worry as much about how the horse stands as how the horse goes. If you want a horse that can show halter and go English, buy one with that in mind. Do not try to create one out of a horse that can trot but lacks correctness.

The shoe should fit the perimeter of the hoof exactly at the toe and toward the middle of the hoof. You should be able to roll a dime along the line where the hoof meets the shoe and not have the dime slip off. A common mistake made by inexperienced or careless farriers is to make the shoes too small. The shoe should be slightly wider than the hoof at the heels and extend back far enough at least to cover the buttress. This will protect the flexor tendons and suspensory ligaments. It is particularly important if the horse lacks good heels.

The hind hooves are shod similar to the front, with the shoe extending one-half to one inch beyond the buttress. This provides support, particularly when the horse is stopping and turning.

If part of the hoof wall is broken or deformed, the shoe should fit through the damaged area like it would have had there been no damage. It may be possible to fill in the lost portion of the wall with acrylics or epoxies.

Six nails are commonly used to fasten the shoe. They should be no lower than three-quarters of an inch above the shoe and usually no higher than one inch. Most professional farriers prefer to nail high. The farrier finishes the hoof by "clinching" the nails, that is, bending the remains of the nail over into the hoof. Clinched nails should look square and feel smooth when you run your fingers over them. The entire hoof should also feel smooth and be free of rasp marks. The periople, the rubbery-feeling area at the hairline of the hoof, should not have been disturbed.

# 16

# Basic Health Care

AS AN OWNER, YOU ARE responsible for the basic health care of your horse. This includes arranging for vaccinations, regular worming, and dental care, and keeping an eye out for any signs of illness. Show horses can be even more prone to illness and stress than the horse that never leaves home because they are hauled great distances, enclosed in trailers for hours at a time and exposed to large numbers of horses and many kinds of illnesses.

It is important for overall health that you establish a regular worming and vaccination schedule with your veterinarian. For each horse, keep a record of what he is given, when, and any adverse reactions he may have had.

# WORMING

A horse should be wormed every sixty days. The most common kinds of worms found in adult horses are large and small strongyles, ascarids, bots, pinworms, tapeworms and stomach worms. Any of these can cause damage, and the degree of severity will depend on the type of worm and the condition the horse is in. Worms may feed on the horse's blood, destroy tissue, obstruct blood vessels, damage organs (including the heart and brain) or consume the food you intended the horse to digest.

Strongyles     There are at least forty different species. The horse becomes infected by consuming the larvae, which came from eggs in the manure of an infected horse. Strongyles may be the most dangerous of the internal parasites. They can cause fever, weight loss, colic, diarrhea and constipation. Some travel extensively through the circulatory system and can affect every organ in the body, including the heart and brain.

Ascarids     Infections occur when the horse consumes eggs that came from the manure of an infected horse. After the eggs are swallowed, the developing embryos penetrate the gut wall and are carried by the bloodstream to the liver and lungs. After about a week, the larvae migrate from the respiratory tract up the trachea to the throat, where they are swallowed again. The worms live to maturity in the small intestine.

Bots     The horse becomes infected by small yellow eggs that were laid on its body by a insect that looks like a bee. The horse ingests the eggs, and they hatch and live in the tongue and cheek for a month before migrating to the stomach, where they feed on blood and tissue for ten to twelve months.

Stomach Worms        These worms can cause gastritis and an upset stomach. Transmitted to the horse by flies, these parasites live primarily in the stomach, but can also affect the lungs and wounds in the skin.

Tapeworms        You'll rarely encounter heavy infestations of tapeworms. The horse becomes infested by swallowing the eggs when grazing in an area that has been infected by the manure of an animal with tapeworms. The worms inhabit the intestines of the horse.

Pinworms        Although common in foals, these worms are found in adult horses as well. Probably the only symptom you will notice is the horse rubbing his tail into a frazzled mess. Pinworms are ingested in water or food and mature in the intestines.

There are a number of ways to get rid of the worms in the horse's body. Dewormers come in granules, powders, liquids and paste. Powders and granules, which are meant to be fed in grain, are effective only if you can get the horse to eat them, and that isn't always easy. Most horses have a truly remarkable talent of being able to eat all of their grain without ingesting the medication you so thoroughly mixed in.

The easiest way to deworm a horse is by using paste, which comes in a plastic syringe that is inserted in the corner of the horse's mouth. Pushing the plunger deposits the paste on the tongue. Once in a while a horse will stick out his tongue and whip the bad-tasting paste onto the stall wall with all the flare of a modern artist, but for most horses paste is the best option available.

Before giving any kind of medication, including dewormer, read the directions. How much of the dewormer you administer depends on the horse's weight. An adult Arabian will weight between 900 and 1,000 pounds. To get a closer estimate of what your horse weighs, get a weight tape from a tack or feed store. The tape should be wrapped around the girth, and the numbers on the tape will provide a weight estimate.

No dewormer on the market can get rid of every type of worm. Effective wormers against strongyles include avermectins, benzimidazoles, and phenylguanidine; against ascarids, piperazine and phenylguanidine; against bots, organophosphates and avermectins; and against tapeworms, pyrantel.

The past ingredient that comes closest to killing all types of worms, except for some stages of ascarids and tapeworms, is ivermectin. Most dewormers kill only those worms in the stomach and intestines at the time the dewormer passes through. Ivermectin eliminates the worms regardless of where they are, and also kills external parasites such as ticks. Because of the way ivermectin works on the parasites, it's unlikely that the parasite will develop a resistance to it. As a precaution, some people make it a practice to rotate types (not just brands) of wormer. If you rotate, make sure you use wormers with active drugs that differ from one another.

Because ivermectin is so effective, tube worming has become practically unnecessary. Tube worming is a procedure performed by a veterinarian in which a tube is passed through the horse's nostril to the stomach, then liquid dewormer is pumped in.

# VACCINATIONS

With show horses, especially, you must be particularly diligent in providing a full range of vaccinations.

Many people give injections themselves without the assistance of a veterinarian. If you want to do this, ask your veterinarian to give you a few lessons first, and make sure you are competent before you give injections without his supervision. Vaccines are injected either into the vein or into the muscle, depending upon what the medication calls for. Some drugs can be fatal if injected in the wrong place.

What vaccinations the horse will need depends on where you live and where the horse will be shipped. Check with a veterinarian and other horse owners to find out what vaccinations are needed. Standard shots are standardly given for the following conditions:

Strangles      Also called distemper, this condition causes abscesses to form in the lymph nodes of the upper respiratory tract. It is highly contagious but rarely fatal. The horse will cough, and swallowing will be painful. When the horse is first vaccinated, it will be given three shots at seven-day intervals. After that, the horse should be vaccinated one to two times a year.

Tetanus     This bacterial infection, found in dirt and manure, enters the horse's body through wounds such as cuts and punctures. It erodes the nerve impulses that direct the movement of muscles. The horse suffers from lockjaw and a general body stiffness. Tetanus is 80 percent fatal, but it can be prevented through regular vaccinations.

After the first vaccination is given, the second follows in four to eight weeks. After that, annual boosters are needed. The vet also may give an injured horse a booster.

Rhino (Rhinopneumonitis)     This viral infection gives the horse a runny nose, congestion, coughing, and an elevated temperature. It may cause mares to abort. Pregnant mares are vaccinated after the second, fifth and seventh months of pregnancy. Other horses receive a first dose, followed by a second four weeks later, and annual to semiannual boosters.

Sleeping Sickness (Encephalomyelitis)     The three viruses of this type are of particular concern: Venezuelan (VEE), Eastern (EEE) and Western (WEE) encephalomyelitis. Ask your veterinarian about what types are a problem in your area. You must vaccinate against each strain to be protected against it.

Encephalomyelitis is transmitted primarily by mosquitoes. An infected horse may act strangely, have a high fever and appear extremely drowsy. Death occurs within five days of his being infected.

Vaccination against EEE and WEE is initially one dose followed by another a week later. The series is repeated annually. VEE vaccinations are given once a year.

Flu (Influenza)     This highly contagious illness usually isn't very serious, but it can be if a secondary infection such as pneumonia sets in. Although the viruses that give horses the flu differ from those that infect human beings, the symptoms are similar: fever, cough and perhaps stiffness, weakness, a runny nose and loss of appetite.

The horse is not going to feel like doing much, and it may take one or two months for him to return to full vigor.

Vaccinating him may save him the discomfort and you the loss of training time. After the initial dose, another is given six to twelve weeks later, followed by annual to semiannual boosters.

# DENTAL CARE

At age three, when many English horses are started under saddle, the horse is still getting his permanent teeth and shedding baby teeth. You may find a chunk of tooth in his feeder. Teeth that do not shed properly can be removed by the vet.

Permanent teeth will continue to come in through ages four and five and will continue to grow throughout the horse's life. Nature intended that the growth rate be matched by the rate the horse wears down the teeth through grazing. However, since the upper and lower teeth do not always align perfectly, sharp spikes may form in areas that are not being worn down evenly.

This painful condition is easily remedied by a veterinarian who "floats the teeth," that is, files down the points. The horse's mouth is usually held open by a device called a gag. How often the teeth need to be floated depends on the horse. Once or twice a year is common, but if the upper and lower teeth match extremely well, a horse may never need this done. If they match poorly, it may have to be done more frequently.

Some of the signs that a horse needs to have his teeth floated include drooling, rolling his food into little balls and making pained facial expressions. Or when he tries to eat grain, it rains down from his mouth. Your horse's dental problems can also cause you big problems as a rider. The bit occupies the space in the gum between the front teeth (the incisors) and back teeth (the premolars and molars). The lone tooth that is in this gum space on each side of the mouth is the canine, which is usually seen only in geldings and stallions.

When a snaffle bit is pulled back, the cheek is forced against the molars. It there is a sharp edge on the molar, it will cause pain and may even cut the cheek. The horse understandably will be fussy in the bridle, and may even throw or shake his head.

Wolf teeth present another dental problem that can affect performance. If your horse has a wolf tooth, you can find it by placing your finger in the gum space, then sliding it back, over the canine, to the first tooth your finger encounters. That tooth will either be a premolar or a wolf tooth. If it looks just like the tooth behind it, it's probably a premolar, and your horse doesn't have wolf teeth. If it looks different from the tooth behind it and is about the same size, it may be a wolf tooth. Wolf teeth can either look like smaller versions of molars or be rounder.

Wolf teeth, like wisdom teeth in human beings, serve no known purpose and sometimes have to be removed. Most adult horses do not even have wolf teeth. Those that do may suffer no discomfort from them, but occasionally they will cause the action of a bit to be painful. When wolf teeth cause problems, they should be removed by a veterinarian.

## SHEATH CARE

The sheath houses the penis. The inside of the sheath secretes a waxy, greasy substance called smegma.

Occasionally the sheath and penis must be cleaned of smegma, but there may also be debris from bedding, dead skin and dirt. If not removed, swelling of the sheath, infection, sores in the sheath or on the penis and difficulty with urination can result. Some horses need their sheaths cleaned as often as several times a month, but all male horses should have it done at least once a year.

Cleaning the sheath is not difficult if the horse cooperates. You can have the vet do it or do it yourself. You may want to have the vet give you a lesson. If the horse is uncooperative or must be drugged, you may want to have the vet clean the sheath.

It is easier to do a thorough job of cleaning the sheath if the penis is extended, but that is not essential. Tranquilizers are usually required to get a gelding to drop his penis; then the penis and sheath are cleaned with a bucket of lukewarm soapy water.

To clean the sheath without getting the horse to extend his penis, use a garden hose connected to lukewarm tap water. Water pressure should be mild. Insert the hose into the sheath a few inches, then gently hold the sheath closed around it so the sheath is extended slightly with water. After a moment, release the sheath and allow the water to flow out. If you do not have a garden hose, a big syringe can be used.

Once the sheath is rinsed, reach inside. Your hand will encounter many folds of skin. Remove the film of smegma covering the sheath and penis. Make sure you have trimmed your fingernails before you do this. Although you can wear gloves, it is easier to use your bare hands because your sense of touch is better. The smegma smells foul and is hard to wash off your hands, but it will come off with soap and warm water.

Soap also will help in removing the smegma from the penis and sheath, but be careful not to use a soap that could irritate the skin or kill the beneficial bacteria that lives in the sheath. Ask your vet to recommend a soap. Rinse the sheath thoroughly to remove any remaining soap.

Another area that must be given attention is a small pouch near the urethra, the tube in the penis through which the urine passes. Smegma accumulates in this pouch, causing a hard deposit called a bean. This must be removed, otherwise it can obstruct urination. The bean usually is soft enough so that you can break it up and work it out with your fingers.

# THE HEALTHY HORSE

In order to know when a horse is ill, you have to know what he is like when he is well. Furthermore, what is normal for one horse might not be for another. An active horse might churn restlessly in his stall but for a quiet horse to do this it may be a sign of distress. Know your horse's behavior and habits. Is he an eager eater or picky? Is he quiet or rambunctious? Does he often lie down, or would that be considered unusual? Does he often paw or pace? What do his legs look and feel like? You should know every contour and bump so you will notice any new swelling, mark or bump. What is the horse's normal temperature, pulse and respiration? If you know what is normal, then you can detect illness.

Temperature        Body temperature ranges between 99°
and 101°F. Arabians tend to have temperatures toward the upper range,
100° to 101° F, but temperatures can vary from horse to horse. Take
the horse's temperature a number of times when he is healthy so you
will know if he has an abnormal temperature when he is ill. The
temperature will also vary according to the amount of work the horse
has just done. During an average workout, the temperature should not
rise above 102.5° F.

Use a livestock thermometer to take a horse's temperature. In one
end of the thermometer is a hole. Thread a string, at least a foot long,
through the hole. The string will help you retrieve the thermometer
from the horse's rectum.

Before inserting the thermometer into the horse's rectum, shake
down the mercury, then coat the thermometer with petroleum jelly
to lessen any possible irritation. Insert at least three-fourths of the
thermometer into the rectum, and leave it there for the length of time
required, usually three minutes. Digital thermometers are faster than
standard thermometers.

Respiration        Normal respiration is relaxed, even and
rhythmic. How many breaths per minute the horse takes varies greatly
according to the task he is performing, but at rest he will take between
ten and fifteen breaths per minute. You can count breaths by watching
his nostrils or sides. The respiration rate can also be increased by things
that are not related to illness, such as exertion, excitement, heat, humid-
ity or obesity.

The horse's lungs hold about thirty quarts of air as compared with
five for human beings. Problems to look for include abnormal sounds
such as rattling, coughing or wheezing; a higher respiration rate;
labored breathing; an uneven breathing rhythm, or more nasal discharge than usual. A small amount of clear discharge is normal and this
may increase with exposure to lots of dust. However, discharge that
is thick or yellow or contains blood are indications of illness.

Pulse        The pulse of a horse at rest is between thirty-
five and forty-five beats per minute. It can accelerate to over a hundred
during exertion. One of the more convenient places to take a pulse is
the artery that runs across the inner surface of the jawbone. Place two

fingers across the artery. Do not use your thumb, or you may confuse the horse's pulse with your own. For one minute, count the number of beats you feel.

# THE ILL HORSE

Any deviation from normal can mean a potential health problem. Keep a record of your horse's health history to enable you to know what's standard and what's a marked change from it.

Listed among your emergency phone numbers should be the number of your regular veterinarian and that of at least one other vet in case the first cannot be reached in an emergency.

When you call the veterinarian, describe the problem calmly, quickly and specifically. Depending on the circumstances, it may help the vet to know if the horse has an abnormal temperature, pulse or respiration and any other signs of distress. Signs of trouble include:

- A temperature below 99° or above 102° F. A low temperature might indicate a number of things, including poisoning, shock from injury, trauma or blood loss. A high temperature indicates fever or that the horse is overheated.
- Hanging the head, depression, loss of appetite, sluggishness.
- Difficulty breathing, coughing, colored nasal discharge and drooling.
- Sounds associated with pain or exertion, such as grunting. Also physical expressions of pain and discomfort.
- A resting pulse of more than fifty beats a minute. This might indicate pain, shock, fever, or dehydration.
- Heat, pain and swelling in any area. This indicates injury there.
- Sweating or shivering for no apparent reason.
- Lying down and refusing to rise.
- Repeated rolling.
- Diarrhea, constipation or blood in the stool. Diarrhea or constipation are not uncommon with changes in feed, but if they come without the feed change, it might be a sign of illness. A dehydrated horse or one with fever will often be constipated.

- Pale gums. Normally the horse's gums are pink, but if the horse is anemic or in shock, they will take on a grayish-pink color.
- Restlessness, pawing.
- Odd positions, such as standing with one or both front legs outstretched. This can be a sign of exhaustion or pain in the front legs.
- Abnormal urine output. Excessive urination can mean kidney problems. Difficulty in urinating can mean an infection in the urinary tract.
- Lack of sounds in the gut. Normally, if you put your ear against the horse's stomach you will hear growling and rumbling sounds. Silence in the gut is an indication of digestive problems, and perhaps colic.

It is up to you to determine if the horse is sufficiently ill to merit calling the veterinarian. Always call the vet if the horse shows signs of great distress or colic.


# FIRST AID

Common sense is the primary requirement of handling equine emergencies. The procedures you follow are similar to those you would use for a person.

You probably will deal with small injuries, such as minor cuts and swellings, yourself. Ask your veterinarian for help in putting together a medical kit that will fit your circumstances and medical knowledge. A standard kit might include:

A reference guide of treatments for equine illnesses and injuries
Antibiotic wound ointment (Have your veterinarian recommend an ointment. You may want to use an ointment that contains fly repellent if flies are a problem)
Mild antiseptic soap for cleaning wounds
An equine thermometer
A roll of sheet cotton
Rolls of gauze

Nonstick wound gauze pads
Vetrap
Adhesive tape
Blunt-end scissors
A fungicide for the variety of funguses, such as ringworm,
horses tend to pick up
Petroleum jelly
Rubbing alcohol

The kit also might include a number of drugs, especially phenylbutazone (bute). Bute, one of the most frequently used drugs on the horse-show circuit, reduces pain and inflammation. It comes in a variety of forms, but most horse owners and trainers, use it in the paste form that is applied with a syringe like the deworming medication.

Another drug commonly found in the medical kit is dimethyl sulphoxide (DMSO). Applied topically, it is rapidly absorbed into the body. DMSO is used to reduce swelling, pain and itching and to speed healing. Because it is so quickly absorbed into the body, it is often used to send other substances, such as bute, into the body. Its quick action can also be a problem, however, because it can draw foreign substances into the body just as easily as it can draw bute or the desired medication. When you use DMSO, wear gloves, and always thoroughly clean the area it will be used on before you apply it. Even then, you never know what the drug may be transporting into the horse's body.

Medical kits also may contain tranquilizers and a whole range of other drugs. Never give the horse a drug unless you are certain it is the right treatment, know the effects and are skilled at administering it. Even so, it is better to consult your veterinarian before giving any drugs.

## EMERGENCY FIRST AID

Most of the health problems your horse will face will be minor and will not require veterinary assistance. Occasionally, however, the illness or injury may be serious enough that you need the veterinarian. Always call the vet in the following instances:

- You don't know what to do.
- There is excessive bleeding or excessive swelling.
- The horse's behavior changes drastically for no apparent reason.
- You suspect colic or founder.
- The horse is going into shock.
- The horse appears to be in great pain.
- The wound, even if it is small, is gaping open and may require stitches to heal without leaving a blemish.

These are emergencies that require immediate veterinary assistance. The more information you can give the veterinarian, the better. When you call, describe the problem. Ask if he or she wants you to take some interim action. In most situations, you should not try to treat the horse until the call has been made to the veterinarian, although if the horse is bleeding, you may want to wipe the blood away to see the extent of the wound. Time spent trying to treat the horse is time lost because the vet could have been on the way to your aid that much sooner. Unless the vet directs you to, don't give the horse any drugs or apply any ointments while waiting. Drugs can confuse diagnosis, and ointments may get in the way if the veterinarian has to suture the wound. Try to keep yourself and the horse calm, and if possible get the horse to a warm, dry, well-lit area in which the veterinarian can work.

Some of the problems you may encounter:

Colic      Show horses tend to be particularly susceptible to colic because of their lifestyles. It can be as mild as a stomachache or serious enough to cause death. If you suspect that a horse is suffering from colic, call the veterinarian immediately. Time is of the essence. While waiting for the veterinarian to arrive, walk the horse to keep it from rolling. Do not administer any drugs. They may confuse the diagnosis.

Causes of colic include intestinal parasites, changes in feed, poor or contaminated feed, sudden diet changes, changes in feeding patterns, drinking large quantities of water after exertion, failure to properly cool off the horse after a hard workout and irregular work patterns, such as working an out-of-condition horse extremely hard infrequently, followed by periods of idleness.

Symptoms include refusal of food or picky eating, restlessness, pawing, rolling and nipping at the abdomen. The horse may pass little or no manure. The sounds in the gut may become louder, softer or be absent entirely. Pulse and respiration will increase. The severe pain may cause the horse to go into shock, and his temperature will drop.

Cuts and Punctures    These are some of the most common equine injuries. When the horse is injured, it may seem that he is bleeding alarming amounts. A horse has about seven gallons of blood in his body. He can lose two to three gallons of blood without serious harm, but if bleeding is extreme or if blood is spurting from the wound (meaning an artery is cut), you have a serious emergency on your hands. Call the veterinarian, then do what you can to control the bleeding.

Use a tourniquet as an absolute last resort, because it can cause extensive damage. Instead of taking that risk, try to control bleeding with direct pressure on the wound or a pressure bandage. Sometime when the vet is at your barn on an nonemergency call, have him or her show you how to apply a pressure bandage to a limb. The first layer is comprised of a nonstick wound pad, followed by a layer each of gauze and cotton, and then Vetrap over the top of that. The procedure is best learned by watching it done, feeling how tight the layers should be, then trying it yourself under supervision. Pressure bandages can help control the bleeding and keep out contaminates such as dirt.

If there is a foreign object in the wound, do not remove it unless there is an overriding reason to do so. Leaving the object in the wound will give the veterinarian an idea of the angle of entry, and what damage it might have caused.

Where there is a lot of bleeding, keep a close eye on the horse. He may go into shock. Shock also may occur in a horse that is very ill or in a great deal of pain. The pulse becomes rapid, reaching eighty beats a minute or more. The horse's temperature and blood pressure drop, and he may break out in a cold sweat. His gums may look white and the membranes in the nose may look bluish. Severe shock can cause death. If the horse shows signs of shock, keep him as quiet, warm and dry as possible while waiting for the veterinarian to arrive.

Founder (Laminitis)    Founder, an inflammation of the sensitive laminae of the foot, can be caused by the horse eating too much grain or fresh green grass, drinking cold water while the body is overheated or by being worked excessively on extremely hard ground. It might affect just the front feet or all four. The horse will appear reluctant to move and may stand with front legs outstretched in an effort to remove weight from the painful front feet. The horse may lie down. The feet will feel hot, and the pulse will pound hard in the blood vessels supplying the feet.

Suspected founder is always an emergency. Call the veterinarian, then slowly walk the horse while you wait. Walking will help the blood circulate in the feet. However, if you suspect the laminitis already has damaged the feet, do not walk the horse more than ten to fifteen minutes in an hour. Further exercise may cause further damage.

It will help the veterinarian to know what the horse is foundering on, and how much he has consumed. If the horse is foundering on grain, do not let him drink water while you're waiting for the vet. Water may make the grain ferment in his stomach, causing even more problems.

Swelling    Ice packs and cold water are the best treatment for swelling. If the swelling is serious enough that you call the vet, do not give the horse any anti-inflammatory medications while you are waiting. They may confuse diagnosis. While waiting, keep the horse as still as possible to prevent further damage to the injured area.

Bowed Tendon    This is an inflammation that causes permanent damage to the tendons that run down the back of the leg—the deep flexor tendon or superficial flexor tendon, or both, usually in a front leg. Bows can be caused by structural defects such as long, weak pasterns that strain the back of the leg, muscle fatigue, being worked hard on ground that provides poor footing or an accidental step that brings too much weight to bear on the tendons.

This can end a horse's show career if the condition is not treated. At the very least, the horse will probably have to be given a year off.

A horse that has bowed a tendon will go lame, and the back of the leg from knee to fetlock will be hot and begin to swell. The more you can keep the swelling down, the better chance the horse will have of recovering.

Wrap the leg tightly with regular leg wraps, and keep the area cold with ice or water. This will keep the swelling down, thus minimizing damage. As you wait for the veterinarian to arrive, keep the horse as still as possible.

If you are away from the barn when the horse bows a tendon, wrap the leg tightly in whatever you can find, even if it means tearing up an article of clothing. Hand walk the horse back to the barn, and call the veterinarian.

Lameness     The causes of lameness are numerous, as are the degrees of how serious the problem may be. Call the vet if the injury to the leg or shoulder appears to be serious, if lameness remains longer than a few days, or if it comes and goes. Lameness is usually not a life-threatening situation, but it can be a serious and lingering problem. The cause of the lameness may be difficult to determine, and even when the horse appears to be sound, he may still be healing. Give him a great deal of rest, and when you return him to work, do so cautiously and slowly, watching for reoccurring lameness. If you have any doubt about how the horse is doing, have him examined by the veterinarian.

A lame horse will have an uneven gait and may rest the sore leg while standing still. He may adopt an awkward or unusual stance, such as standing with one front leg extended. Some horses tend to favor such poses even when they are not lame. Look for stances that are not usual for your horse.

It is more likely that the horse will show the lameness in motion rather than standing. Observe the horse trotting over a level surface. A horse with a lame front leg will bob his head up when the sore leg strikes the ground. The horse also may shorten the stride of the sore leg. If the hind leg is sore, the shortening of one stride may be one of the few gait disturbances you see. The horse with a lame hind leg may move unbalanced behind, may appear to he holding one side of his rump higher than the other or may try to take skipping steps on one side.

# 17

# Feeding

THE SUBJECT OF FEEDS AND feeding tends to bore even the most ardent horseman. Information about DE (digestible energy), TDN (total digestible nutrients), Ca:P ratios (calcium to phosphorus) and percentages of this and that can be overwhelming when all you really want to know is how much grain to put in the coffee can and how much hay to throw in the manger.

By following a few basic guidelines, however, you can feed your horse properly without having to use a calculator to figure out TDNs or DEs. Think of food as energy. You've already done this if you've ever been on a diet and thought, If I do four minutes of aerobics, I can burn off that marshmallow I ate. Calories are just units of energy, for the horse also. The amount of feed he gets depends on his size and the amount of work he does. In other words, how much grain is the horse going to burn off during his aerobics?

Within the amount of food you give the horse must be all the nutrients he needs. Most horse feeds are already fairly well balanced and complement each other. That's why even if you just gave food to the horse without any content planning, no dire consequences would result. The horse may not be as healthy as he could be or have as shiny a coat, but if you use a little common sense and do not go to extremes in feeding, you will not do serious, long-range damage.

In the feeding schedule I suggest, hay will be used to maintain basic weight and functioning and grain for the extra energy that will be burned off in workouts.

# HAY

How much hay to feed depends on how much the horse weighs. A 1,000-pound horse will maintain his weight well on around 15 pounds of hay a day. A commonly used formula is to feed 1½ to 2 pounds of hay for every 100 pounds the horse weighs. As discussed in an earlier chapter, it is fairly easy to find out how much the horse weighs. You can buy a special measuring tape that goes around the girth and gives an approximate weight.

Feeding by weight doesn't mean you have to be out there every morning weighing hay and give up the flake system. When you get a new shipment of hay, weigh a few flakes until you are able to approximate weights just by looking. A flake of alfalfa is going to weigh more than a flake of grass hay. The amount you feed should be based on the weight, not the size, of the flake. Once you can approximate how much a flake of a certain hay will weigh, you're set until you get another shipment of hay. When it arrives, weigh a few more flakes, because the weight of hay can vary from shipment to shipment.

You really can't get into trouble by overfeeding hay. There is no such thing as a "hay belly." Hay is not the primary culprit of a round belly. Lack of exercise is.

The kind of hay you use will depend on where you live and what you have access to. You're probably feeding alfalfa, clover, grass or a grass/alfalfa mix. With any type of hay, select bales that smell good, are leafy (see page 187), show good color inside the bale and are not dusty, moldy or full of weeds. Some weeds are toxic or have stickers that can lodge in the gums (see page 187). Horse owners in the Midwest, South, Southwest and East must also beware of blister beetles in hay. They are highly toxic to horses.

Good hay is leafy and shows good color. This hay is much too stemmy.

Avoid hay that contains lots of stickers such as these, which can get stuck in the horse's gums.

One of the nice things about hay is that most types have a similar energy content. Alfalfa and clover have a bit more energy to offer than grass hays, but not a great deal more. They do, however, vary in protein, vitamins, minerals and nutrients.

The body needs protein to maintain and replace cells. Nearly 9 percent of the horse's diet should be protein. That is not a difficult requirement to meet if the horse is receiving legume hays (clover or alfalfa). Legumes easily meet the requirement even if no grain is fed. Grass hay, on the other hand, contains less protein than the horse needs. A horse eating only grass hay can develop a protein deficiency. The grass hay should be supplemented with grain.

All of the hays provide the necessary vitamins, although grass hay tends to be a little short on the B vitamin thiamine. Thiamine helps the horse metabolize carbohydrates. Again, you can make up the shortage with grain.

All of the hay may also be short on vitamin A. Vitamin A plays many roles in the body, including aiding in healthy skin and mucous membranes and in fertility. A horse eating recently harvested hay gets an adequate supply of vitamin A, but the longer the hay sits in storage, the less it has to offer. The hay does not really contain vitamin A but carotene, which the horse's body converts to vitamin A. Always buy hay from the current season, instead of that from seasons past. The freshest hay will be higher in carotene.

Grass and legume hay part company when it comes to minerals. Grass has all its minerals in proper balance. That's fine if you are only feeding grass hay, but if you add the grain you need to boost the protein content, you are also throwing off the mineral balance. Legume hay starts out unbalanced and is brought back into balance by the grain.

The balance involves two minerals, phosphorus and calcium. Hay in general provides an adequate amount of all of the other minerals. Phosphorus and calcium, however, present more of a challenge. The horse needs to receive each in certain amounts. If he receives too much calcium, he won't absorb enough phosphorus, and vice versa. Your own body is the same way. With these two minerals, the body acts like a motel, renting out rooms on a first come, first-served basis. It rents rooms to whoever shows up first, and when guests come along later who really need a place to stay, no rooms are left.

Ideally in the body's motel, two rooms would be rented out to calcium guests for every one room rented to phosphorus guests. But the body is too busy filling up the rooms to notice who is staying in them. You have to make sure a balance is struck.

If you want to feed the well-balanced grass hay, but need the extra boost of the protein and energy of grain, buy a commercial grain mix that has been balanced (see below). It should state if it is balanced or not on the label. Another possibility would be to add a calcium supplement to the grain to balance the phosphorus in the grain. Your feed store or veterinarian can help you determine the right amount of calcium to add to the grain you are buying.

Alfalfa and clover hay are excellent in feeding programs that use grain. The legumes are calcium heavy and thus work well when fed with the phosphorus-heavy grains. Alfalfa is a popular hay that is available in most places; it has a little more energy and quite a bit more protein to offer the horse. But don't feed legume hay for an extended period of time if that is all the horse is eating. It should be accompanied by grain (just how much will be discussed shortly) or be mixed with grass hay. I prefer to use an alfalfa/grass mix. It is a little high in calcium when fed alone but is within acceptable limits and will provide adequate nutrition and energy.

A mixed, balanced grain.

When your English horse is not being worked, just give him hay. If you can't handle the disappointment in his face when he sees he's not getting any grain, toss a chopped-up carrot in his bucket, or just give him a handful of grain. He does not need grain unless he is expending the extra energy. If you feed around 15 pounds of hay, such as an alfalfa/grass mix, the horse will get everything he needs without your having to worry about adding anything else to the diet.

# PASTURE

Pasture grass is rich in vitamins and minerals and comes closest to what nature intended the horse's diet should be—if the pasture is green and in good condition. Pastures that are dry or brown from the winter cold are low in protein, phosphorus and energy. Green pastures may also be low in phosphorus, and pastures that are grazed down cannot adequately supply the needs of the horse.

If the pasture is in good shape, it should do fairly well supplying the needs of the idle horse. You may want to set out a pasture supplement block, which is designed especially to make up for whatever the pasture is lacking. When you put your horse to work, however, he is going to need more than just pasture to boost his energy levels. Add grain to his diet.

# GRAINS

An English horse on a standard exercise program needs more high energy than hay will give him. He cannot eat enough hay to fulfill his needs. Hay will fill him up first, but he needs a concentrated source of energy—grain.

But use the grain conservatively. Too much grain can cause founder, colic and problems in the bones and joints. It is better to feed the horse too little grain than too much.

Feed grain by weight. People who use coffee cans to measure out grain can get confused, thinking, Well, it's a ten-pound coffee can, so if I fill it to the top I'm feeding ten pounds. That's only true if you're feeding your horse coffee grounds. Grains vary greatly in weight. A can of corn will weigh considerably more than a can of oats. The weight of the grain will even vary from batch to batch. If the oats came from an area that received little rain, they are going to be lighter, with less grain in the hulls, than if they came from an area with better growing conditions. When you get a new batch of grain, weigh a scoop of it to see how much you should feed. You can still use your favorite coffee can, just know how much a can of grain really weighs.

The grain should smell good and be free of mold and foreign objects like rocks. Whether you select whole, rolled or crimped grains is a matter of individual preferences. Some people contend that when the hull is broken by processing nutrients are lost. Others say processing makes the grain more digestible. One study found that processing increases the feed value of grains from 2 to 9 percent.

The grain you select will be dictated by availability, price and the hay you are complementing. The major grains used are corn, oats and barley. Corn is the leader in providing the most concentrated energy, followed by barley, then oats. For example, if you switch to corn from another grain but want about the same energy level, you would feed slightly less corn than the other grain.

Oats is the safest of the grains to feed because it packs less energy, and the bulk of the hulls provides fiber, giving you some margin for feeding errors. Oats and barley are among the highest protein grains, making them good grains to feed with grass hay to offset the low-protein level in the hay. However, if you feed them with grass hay, you should still add calcium to balance out the phosphorus in the grain. Barley is a little higher in phosphorus than oats. An easier route when looking for a grain to feed with grass hay is to give the horse a mixed feed that is already balanced or to give the horse alfalfa/grass hay with oats or barley. The oats or barley will compensate for the protein lacking in the grass, and the alfalfa will compensate for the abundance of phosphorus in the grain.

Corn is the lowest in protein of the three grains, so in general is not the best grain to feed with grass. It is, however, a good complement to legume hays. Oats and barley also complement the legume hays well.

Determine how much grain to give the horse by how much work he does, how intense the workout is, and how large he is. A 1,000-pound adult horse that works at a moderate pace should receive around

1 to 1½ pounds of oats for every half hour of work. For barley, give him slightly less, and corn, still less.

"Moderate" for an English horse is a reasonably casual workout. When you really demand the ultimate effort from him, he's going to need more energy. For every half hour of high-energy work, feed 2 to 4 pounds, and more if he needs it.

As you increase the pounds of grain given, lower the amount of hay feed. Twelve to 13 pounds of hay are usually adequate for a horse consuming 3 to 4 pounds of grain. However, never let the pounds of grain you feed exceed the pounds of hay. Grain should not equal more than half of the total pounds of food the horse consumes. His digestive system cannot handle that much concentrated feed. It needs the fiber offered by the hay to function properly.

The horse's physical condition will tell you if you are feeding him properly. If you are giving him more than he can burn off in exercise, he will get fat. If you're not giving him enough, he will become skinny and may run out of energy during the workouts, or sink into deep exhaustion as soon as you dismount. Also take into consideration the horse's activity level in his stall or pasture. If he's the busy type, he is going to need more feed than the horse that just stands around.

# ELECTROLYTES

Electrolytes are salts in the horse's body. If the electrolyte level becomes too low, the horse will become dehydrated and may suffer muscle cramps and other problems. Buying him a salt block and providing him with an adequate diet is enough to keep electrolytes in balance under normal circumstances.

Electrolytes are lost through sweat. Some horse owners feed electrolytes in the hot summer months when the horses regularly become soaking wet with sweat during workouts. Electrolytes can be purchased in powder form to add to grain, or in liquid form to put in water. Follow the directions on the label, or have your veterinarian help you establish an appropriate amount to give. If you put the electrolytes in water, also provide a bucket of pure water so the horse is not forced to take in more electrolytes than he wants. Excessive amounts of electrolytes can cause problems.

# VITAMIN AND MINERAL SUPPLEMENTS

Most nutritional authorities say that horses generally do not need vitamin and mineral supplements. Most barns use supplements with zeal, however. Dietitians say vitamin supplements are unnecessary, yet many people take them anyway.

If you are concerned that the horse isn't getting sufficient minerals, buy him a mineralized salt block and let him choose how much to consume.

If you want to feed a vitamin supplement, or a vitamin and mineral supplement, chose carefully. You may even want to have your vet recommend one appropriate for the needs of your horse. What supplement to chose may also be influenced by where you live. In the Northwest, many horse owners feed a supplement containing selenium because that mineral is needed in small amounts but feed grown in the region does not produce sufficient amounts of it. In other parts of the country, this is not a problem. It would be unnecessary, and perhaps dangerous, to feed a supplement with selenium. The horse's body stores selenium, and too much can be toxic.

The horse's body also stores some vitamins: A, D and E remain in the body until they are used, others are excreted if the horse does not need them. Most supplements contain A and D and sometimes E in small amounts. If you feed a supplement, follow the directions on the package. Giving the horse too much can cause an unhealthy buildup of the stored vitamins and minerals.

# WATER

The horse should always have access to clean, clear water except during the cooling-down period directly after a workout. Keep the water container clean and free of algae. Water buckets and automatic waterers in stalls should be cleaned at least once a week, particularly if your horse gets grain and hay into his water, where they can stagnate. If his water looks like something you would not want to drink, he should not have to drink it either.

# SHINING THROUGH

A shiny coat comes more from what you put inside the horse than what you apply on the outside. Sound nutrition and the oils in the grain you feed him will give his coat a healthy shine. Some owners also sprinkle on top of the grain a little linseed meal, soybean oil meal or a few tablespoons of corn oil. The oil aids in preventing dry hair and encourages shine.

In addition to diet, the coat's shine is brought out by brushing and by protecting it from sun damage. Horses in pasture full time cannot avoid some sun damage, but the part-time pasture horse can. If your horse gets out for a few hours a day, turn him out in the early morning or at dusk to lessen the sun's impact. If it is not too hot, you can put a sheet on him.

# FEEDING SCHEDULE

The horse's digestive system was designed for a grazing animal that spends most of the day eating. It was never meant to take in a large amount of food in the morning, fast through the day and then receive another large amount of food in the evening.

The best feeding schedule is frequent and regular. Feed the horse the same amount and at the same times, even when you are at shows. Most people feed in the morning and in the evening because it is convenient for them. But feeding more frequently, by giving the horse smaller amounts three to four times a day, is better for his digestive system and may make him less prone to digestive problems.

After the horse has eaten, wait one to two hours before working him hard. If you work him before feeding him, make sure he has cooled out before he eats.

When changing feed, such as from alfalfa to clover, do it gradually, mixing in a little of the new feed with the old over the span of a few days until the transition is complete.

# ACCOMMODATIONS

Regardless of where you keep your horse, whether it is in a stall or pasture, it should be clean and hazard free.

Clean the stall at least once a day because wet bedding is uncomfortable for the horse to lie down in, and it also promotes hoof problems and attracts flies. Inspect the stall regularly for protruding nails, loose boards, and anything else that poses the risk of injury to your horse. All surfaces should be smooth, without sharp edges. Buckets, if they are not attached to the wall, should have their handles removed so the horse cannot get a leg through them. If the buckets are attached to the wall, the attachments should be rounded, without any edges to hurt the horse. Buckets should be wide enough for the horse to get his face into easily.

The manger, if it is at ground level, should have solid sides. A rolling horse can get his leg caught in a slotted manger. Metal mangers that hang on the wall should be solid and free of protrusions and sharp edges.

A good, sound fence.

The stall itself should be large enough for the horse to lie down and stretch out easily. It should be light and well ventilated. When going into the barn, you should not feel like you've descended into a dungeon. Your horse deserves better. Windows should be the kind that can be closed in the winter to keep out drafts. Doorways should be wide and walls should be solid enough to sustain the kick of a horse.

Ideally the horse should have access to the outside. Turn out daily in a paddock or pasture if at all possible. It will do wonders for his mind.

The pasture or paddock should have a well-maintained, hazard-free fence (see page 195)—no wire, nothing protruding, nothing that will ensnare the horse. Even smooth electric wire can cut the horse.

Within the fence should be lots of safe, open space. Horses can be amazingly creative when it comes to getting injured. I've patched up wounds that just a day before I would not have believed it possible for the horse to sustain. Regularly check for hazards—stray nails, loose fencing, toxic plants, tree limbs, ditches or ruts, sprinklers—it's your job to look out for your horse's safety.

Remove from the pasture all of the weeds the horse cannot or should not eat; fertilize and water the pasture regularly. It also is important to keep both the paddock and pasture clean. Raking up the manure is important for hygiene as well as pest control.

# 18

# Stress

WHEN IT COMES TO stress, show horses are the Wall Street executives of the equine world. They operate under tremendous strain that can threaten their mental and physical well-being.

All animals experience stress. It is a physical response intended to boost the animal's ability to protect himself. In the face of danger, chemicals enter the bloodstream, increasing the pulse, respiration and blood sugar. Arteries widen to send more blood to the waiting muscles. A horse, then, is ready for instant action to flee from a predator or to defend himself.

But the stress response is blind. It can't distinguish between the threat of a predator and anxiety from an overlong trailer ride. For each situation, the response is the same: pumping out chemicals to help the horse flee for his life. Stress can build up in the body—human and equine—causing a host of problems. Executives get ulcers. Your horse may develop nervous habits or, like the executive, health problems.

In his natural state, the horse roams unconfined in large herds. Compared to this existence, most show horses live unnatural lives. They are confined alone in stalls, hauled great distances, ridden and subjected to shifting schedules. To keep your horse happy and healthy, be on the lookout for symptoms of stress. They may be your first indication of more serious problems ahead. Following are some stress-related problems to watch for.

## STALL VICES

Remember that the stress response is geared to stimulate the horse into physical action. The action, when taken, alleviates the tension by burning the products of the stress response. The executive, after gulping his or her antacids, might ease the stress with a round of golf. But the horse confined to a stall may not be able to burn off the stress physically. His need for action will be frustrated by confinement, creating more stress as his body demands that he do something. If this continues, your horse will find a solution of his own for releasing the tension. He may develop stall vices, such as constantly weaving back and forth, chewing wood, pacing or windsucking.

Windsucking is an addictive behavior in which the horse fastens his teeth on something, then pulls back, causing air to rush down his throat. Researchers at the Tufts University School of Veterinary Medicine in Medford, Massachusetts, have found that windsucking may cause the release of chemical substances in the brain that create a high, like that experienced by a drug user.

Windsucking is difficult to treat. Usually the horse is made to wear a tight metal collar, but the Tufts University researchers have found that certain drugs are successful in treating windsucking. You will want to consult with your veterinarian if your horse has this problem.

## PHYSICAL RAMIFICATIONS

Stress can cause any number of physical problems. Your horse may be more prone to colic and suffer from other digestive disorders. The constant strain may affect his ability to fight illness, so he may become ill more easily and not recover as quickly. He may also become run down, tire more easily and become cranky and depressed.

The horse's performance in the ring may suffer as it becomes harder for him to endure the strain. The brightness and perky, ears-forward attitude will be gone. Instead of settling down and responding to the rider's commands when pressed to do more, the horse may blow up or become so tense and confused that he cannot do anything right. He may sweat prematurely, his pulse may race, his respiration rate may rise. Even simple tasks may become more difficult for him. As his performance worsens, the rider will press him harder to keep him at a competitive level. Eventually, if the stress is not relieved, he will burn out. The years of training that went into making him into a show horse will be wasted.

As the guardian of your horse's health, it is up to you to prevent him from suffering the equivalent of an equine nervous breakdown.

## DEFENSES AGAINST STRESS

Exercise    The first line of defense is exercise; it will alleviate stress, tone the horse's body and make him feel happier and healthier. Allowing him to be turned loose in a paddock or pasture to play, roll in the dirt and wander about is good for his mind and body. The more time he can spend outside with room to roam, the better.

More organized forms of exercise will be needed to keep him in shape. It is better if riding can be both in the arena and outside in a less formal setting to keep him bright. Training puts stress on the horse, but some stress is necessary. No one's life, including a horse's, can be stress free. Without some stress, it probably would be difficult to get the horse to do much of anything. Good training techniques will channel the stress to achieve heightened performance. Poor training techniques will do just the opposite—create stress and confusion at the same time, thus compounding the existing stress instead of relieving or channeling it. Another example of unproductive stress is caused by pushing the horse too hard too soon or asking him to do a task he is physically unable to perform.

Entertainment      Most show horses spend enormous amounts of time in their stalls. (This could be likened to locking yourself in a room for days with nothing but food and bedding.) Consequently the horse has little to do to entertain himself and burn off the stress. Faced with the need for action or to relieve boredom, the horse will do what he can to keep himself amused. This is how stable vices begin.

Giving the horse toys can help him work off excess energy and occupy his time. If you watch him in his stall, you may notice him already playing with his buckets, and anything else in the stall. There are a variety of horse toys on the market, but anything that the horse can bat around and chew on will work just as well. Plastic milk bottles work very well loose in the stall or suspended on a string from the rafters. Don't leave the cap on the bottle because the horse could swallow it.

Whatever you give the horse must be safe—nothing that he can swallow, cut himself on or ingest that would be toxic. Scrutinize any toy the way you would if you were giving it to an infant. One trainer who gave his horse highway department road pylons ended up with a horse with bone chips in his knee. The horse loved playing with the pylons, and would swing them around vigorously, occasionally hitting the hard edges against his legs, causing him to fall down. While it was never determined what exactly caused the bone chips, the pylons were suspect.

Companionship      To meet the horse's need for company, some owners buy their horses pets, such as goats. The pet lives in the stall with the horse and travels to shows with him. Some horses "adopt" pets, such as barn cats and dogs, and become quite attached to them.

Easing Show Stress      A horse show can be the ultimate in stress. The horse spends hours on end in a claustrophobic trailer. At the show he is surrounded by the unfamiliar; is one day in the stall, then the next day is ridden long, hard and at peculiar hours; is kept awake by strange sounds, partying people and barn lights that stay on all night. He may also be fed at unusual times.

Some horses accept all of this willingly and only become tired or cranky toward the end of the show. Other horses find this a traumatic experience. In either case, you can make the show considerably less stressful. Begin by following your horse's regular feeding schedule as much as possible. If he's used to getting fed at 8:00 A.M. and 5:00 P.M., make every effort to keep to those times unless participation in a class prevents it. Rather than buying food at the show, give him the same feed he gets at home. If it is extremely hot at the show, you may want to add a sprinkle of salt to his water to combat dehydration. The salt may cause him to drink more and retain more water.

At the larger shows, it's not uncommon to see someone practicing at two in the morning, for a variety of reasons, among them avoiding crowded arenas and the watchful eyes of competitors. Whether it is worth the effort is up to the rider, but remember that these are the hours the horse is usually asleep. If you keep your horse up late, make sure he has ample opportunity during the day to sleep. He may have difficulty sleeping at the show anyway because of the activity at all hours and classes that may be very early or very late in the day.

It may help the horse get his sleep if you cover his stall with curtains during the evening and morning hours to cut down on the distractions. You might also want to remove the light bulb above the stall at night.

If the horse is not going to be ridden daily, bring along his stall toys, and take him out for relaxed walks. This will relieve stress and help him get used to the clamor of show life. In general, the more he can get out and about, the better. When you bathe him and time permits, walk him dry rather than drying him in the stall. When cooling the horse out after a workout, hand walk him and let him relax. Do what you can to relieve him of the monotony and strain of the show.

When you ride or handle the horse, behave in a calm and quiet manner. Horses are sensitive to the rider's emotions. If classes make you nervous, take a few deep breaths and calm yourself down before getting on the horse. Concentrate on your job as the rider to hold your nervousness at bay.

When you are in the ring, you should behave in a professional manner, riding the horse to the best of your ability whether you are a trainer or not. Do not ride when you are angry. It communicates tension, your skills may not be at their best and you may take your anger out on the horse. You also should not ride if you have been drinking or are on any medication that could blur your judgment.

Impaired judgment can result in injury to yourself or the horse, or at the very least cause setbacks in the horse's training.

If you want the horse to give you his best, you have to give him yours.

To the horse, you are coach, companion, beautician, nurse and the beloved chef who brings his chow. That is not something to be taken lightly. Each of those roles have equal importance in his life, and his success as an English horse. A horse that is coached poorly cannot succeed, despite tremendous talent. But talent and training are useless if the horse is too undernourished, stressed, ill or injured to perform. He can't run just on raw desire, any more than you can make him win with wishes.

Success is earned through the daily efforts that over time come together to make a whole. It is like building a bridge to where you want to be. If even one piece is missing, the bridge can't be crossed.

# INDEX

Numerals in *italics* indicate illustrations.